# PERFORMANCE

## FAITH AT WORK

### *AT A GLANCE*


| SESSION | REFERENCE | SUBJECT | PAGE |
|---|---|---|---|
| **1** | James 1:1–11 | Salutation & Trials | 10 |
| **2** | James 1:12–18 | Trials & Temptations | 14 |
| **3** | James 1:19–27 | Listening & Doing | 18 |
| **4** | James 2:1–13 | Favoritism Forbidden | 22 |
| **5** | James 2:14–26 | Faith & Deeds | 26 |
| **6** | James 3:1–12 | Taming the Tongue | 30 |
| **7** | James 3:13–18 | Kinds of Wisdom | 34 |
| **8** | James 4:1–12 | Submit to God | 38 |
| **9** | James 4:13–17 | Boasting | 42 |
| **10** | James 5:1–6 | Warning to the Rich | 46 |
| **11** | James 5:7–12 | Patience in Suffering | 50 |
| **12** | James 5:13–20 | Prayer of Faith | 54 |


**Serendipity House / P.O. Box 1012 / Littleton, CO 80160**
TOLL FREE 1-800-525-9563 / www.serendipityhouse.com

SECOND EDITION
01 02 03 04 / **201 series • CHG** / 10 9 8 7 6

**PROJECT ENGINEER:**
Lyman Coleman

**WRITING TEAM:**
Richard Peace, Lyman Coleman, Matthew Lockhart, Andrew Sloan, Cathy Tardif

**PRODUCTION TEAM:**
Christopher Werner, Sharon Penington, Erika Tiepel

**COVER PHOTO:**
© 1998 Warren Morgan / Westlight

## CORE VALUES

**Community:** The purpose of this curriculum is to build community within the body of believers around Jesus Christ.

**Group Process:** To build community, the curriculum must be designed to take a group through a step-by-step process of sharing your story with one another.

**Interactive Bible Study:** To share your "story," the approach to Scripture in the curriculum needs to be open-ended and right brain—to "level the playing field" and encourage everyone to share.

**Developmental Stages:** To provide a healthy program in the life cycle of a group, the curriculum needs to offer courses on three levels of commitment: (1) Beginner Stage—low-level entry, high structure, to level the playing field; (2) Growth Stage—deeper Bible study, flexible structure, to encourage group accountability; (3) Discipleship Stage—in-depth Bible study, open structure, to move the group into high gear.

**Target Audiences:** To build community throughout the culture of the church, the curriculum needs to be flexible, adaptable and transferable into the structure of the average church.

## ACKNOWLEDGMENTS

To Zondervan Bible Publishers
for permission to use
the NIV text,
*The Holy Bible, New International Bible Society.*

# Questions & Answers

STAGE

**1.** ***What stage in the life cycle of a small group is this course designed for?***

Turn to the first page of the center section of this book. There you will see that this 201 course is designed for the second stage of a small group. In the Serendipity "Game Plan" for the multiplication of small groups, your group is in the Growth Stage.

GOALS

**2.** ***What are the goals of a 201 study course?***

As shown on the second page of the center section (page M2), the focus in this second stage is equally balanced between Spiritual Formation, Group Building, and Mission / Multiplication.

BIBLE STUDY

**3.** ***What is the approach to Bible Study in this course?***

Take a look at page M3 of the center section. The objective in a 201 course is to discover what a book of the Bible, or a series of related Scripture passages, has to say to our lives today. We will study each passage seriously, but with a strong emphasis on practical application to daily living.

FOUR-STAGE LIFE CYCLE OF A GROUP

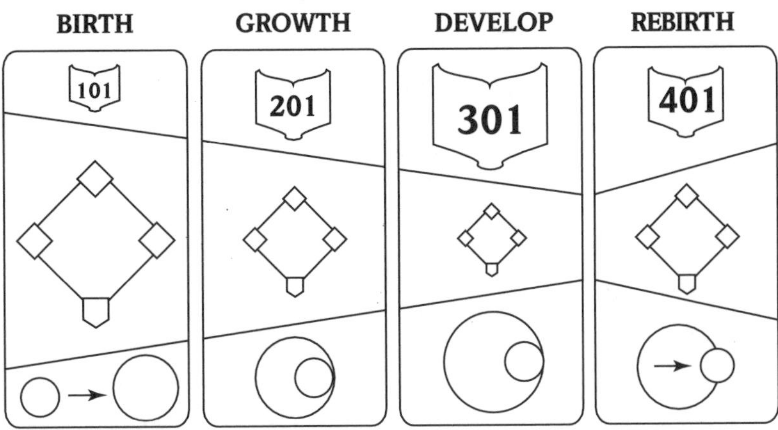

GROUP BUILDING

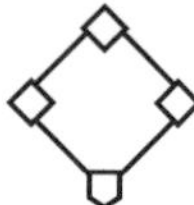

**4.** ***What is the meaning of the baseball diamond on pages M2 and M3 in relation to Group Building?***

Every Serendipity course includes group building. First base is where we share our own stories; second base means affirming one another's stories; third base is sharing our personal needs; and home plate is deeply caring for each others' needs. In this 201 course we will continue "checking in" with each other and holding each other accountable to live the Christian life.

MISSION / MULTIPLICATION

**5.** ***What is the mission of a 201 group?***

The mission of this 201 Covenant group is to discover the future leaders for starting a new group. (See graph on the previous page.) During this course, you will be challenged to identify three people and let this team use the Bible Study time to practice their skills. The center section will give you more details.

THE EMPTY CHAIR

**6.** ***How do we fill "the empty chair"?***

First, pull up an empty chair during the group's prayer time and ask God to bring a new person to the group to fill it. Second, have everyone make a prospect list of people they could invite and keep this list on their refrigerator until they have contacted all those on their list.

AGENDA

**7.** ***What is the agenda for our group meetings?***

A three-part agenda is found at the beginning of each session. Following the agenda and the recommended amount of time will keep your group on track and will keep the three goals of Spiritual Formation, Group Building, and Mission / Multiplication in balance.

## SUBGROUPING

If you have nine or more people at a meeting, Serendipity recommends you divide into groups of 4–6 for the Bible Study. Count off around the group: "one, two, one, two, etc."—and have the "ones" move quickly to another room for the Bible Study. Ask one person to be the leader and follow the directions for the Bible Study time. After 30 minutes, the Group Leader will call "Time" and ask all subgroups to come together for the Caring Time.

**ICE-BREAKERS**

8. ***How do we decide what ice-breakers to use to begin the meetings?***

Page M7 of the center section contains an index of ice-breakers in four categories: (1) those for getting acquainted in the first session or when a new person comes to a meeting; (2) those for the middle sessions to help you report in to your group; (3) those for the latter sessions to affirm each other and assign roles in preparation for starting a new group in the future; and (4) those for evaluating and reflecting in the final session.

**GROUP COVENANT**

9. ***What is a group covenant?***

A group covenant is a "contract" that spells out your expectations and the ground rules for your group. It's very important that your group discuss these issues—preferably as part of the first session (see also page M32 in the center section).

**GROUND RULES**

10. ***What are the ground rules for the group?*** (Check those you agree upon.)

❐ PRIORITY: While you are in the course, you give the group meetings priority.

❐ PARTICIPATION: Everyone participates and no one dominates.

❐ RESPECT: Everyone is given the right to their own opinion and all questions are encouraged and respected.

❐ CONFIDENTIALITY: Anything that is said in the meeting is never repeated outside the meeting.

❐ EMPTY CHAIR: The group stays open to new people at every meeting.

❐ SUPPORT: Permission is given to call upon each other in time of need—even in the middle of the night.

❐ ADVICE GIVING: Unsolicited advice is not allowed.

❐ MISSION: We agree to do everything in our power to start a new group as our mission (see center section).

# Introduction to James

## Authorship

In the New Testament, there are apparently four men by the name of James, but only two who might conceivably have written this epistle—either James the apostle, or James the Just, the half-brother of Jesus. Since it is almost certain that James the apostle (the son of Zebedee) was killed by Herod in A.D. 44 (before the epistle could have been written), traditionally the author has been assumed to be James, the leader of the church in Jerusalem and the brother of Jesus (Mark 6:3).

The pilgrimage of James to faith is fascinating. At first Jesus' family was hostile to his ministry (John 7:5) and, in fact, tried to stop it at one point (Mark 3:21). Yet after Jesus' ascension, Jesus' mother and brothers are listed among the early believers (Acts 1:14). For James, this coming to faith may have resulted from Jesus' postresurrection appearance to him (1 Cor. 15:7).

Apart from the fact that they were closely related, James' relationship to Jesus is not totally clear. Some maintain that they were cousins (the New Testament word for "brother" is looser in meaning than the modern equivalent). Some suggest he was a half-brother to Jesus, a son of Mary and Joseph. Others say that James might have been an older stepbrother of Jesus by a (conjectural) marriage of Joseph previous to his marriage to Mary. The latter view (which excludes any blood relationship to Jesus), might better explain the failure of Jesus' brother to believe in him during his lifetime (Mark 3:21; John 7:2–8). And a lack of concern for Mary (because she was only their stepmother) might also explain why Jesus, from the cross, committed his mother to the apostle John (John 19:25–27). But the reason may have been that Mary's discipleship alienated her from her other children, who still did not believe in Jesus (Robert H. Gundry, *A Survey of the New Testament,* p. 324).

## A Church Leader

In any case, James emerged as the leader of the church in Jerusalem. It was to James that Peter reported after his miraculous escape from Herod's prison (Acts 12:17). James presided over the first Jerusalem Council, which decided the important question of whether to admit Gentiles to the church (Acts 15, especially vv. 13–21). James was consulted by Paul during his first trip to Jerusalem after his conversion (Gal. 1:19), and then James joined in the official recognition of Paul's call as Apostle to the Gentiles (Gal. 2:8–10). It is to James that Paul later brought the collection for the poor (Acts 21:17–25).

## A Jew

We also know that James was a strict Jew who adhered to the Mosaic Law (Gal. 2:12), yet unlike the Judaizers, he supported Paul's ministry to the Gentiles (Acts 21:17–26). Later accounts indicate that James was martyred in A.D. 62.

The question of who wrote the book of James is still, however, somewhat of a puzzle, primarily because Jesus and his saving work is mentioned so little—a curious omission if the author was Jesus' brother. This question baffled even the ancient church. Both the Latin Father Jerome and the church historian Eusebius (as well as others) observe that not all accept James as having been written by our Lord's brother.

## Audience

James is one of the General Epistles (along with 1 and 2 Peter, John's epistles, and Jude), so called because it has no single destination. Thus, it is not clear to whom James is addressing his comments. At first glance, it appears that he is writing to Jewish Christians dispersed around the Greek world: "To the twelve tribes scattered among the nations" (1:1). But since

Peter uses the same sort of inscription (1 Peter 1:1–2) when he is clearly addressing Gentile Christians (who consider themselves the new Israel), James' destination remains unclear. In fact, a strong case can be made (see Sophie Laws, *The Epistle of James: Harper New Testament Commentaries*, pp. 32–38) that James was writing for a community of "God-fearers," that is, Gentiles who had been deeply attracted to Judaism. That such folk were then drawn to Christianity is clear from examples in Acts, such as Cornelius (Acts 10:2,22), Lydia (Acts 16:14), Titius Justus (Acts 18:7), and others. This would help to explain the convergence of Jewish, Greek and Christian elements in the book of James.

### Date

It is difficult to date the book of James. Some place it very early, around A.D. 45, making it the first New Testament book. Others date it quite late.

### Characteristics

Among the New Testament books, James is an oddity. It is written in quite a different style from the others, more like the book of Proverbs than Paul's epistles. But even more than its style, its contents set James apart. It does not treat many of those themes we have come to expect in the New Testament.

### Its Omissions

There is no mention of the Holy Spirit, and no reference to the redemptive work or resurrection of Christ. In fact, it contains only two references to the name Jesus Christ (1:1 and 2:1). Furthermore, when examples are given, they are drawn from the lives of Old Testament prophets, not from the experiences of Jesus. Although the title *Lord* appears 11 times, it generally refers to the name of God and not to Jesus. Indeed, it is God the Father who is the focus in the book of James.

Thus, Martin Luther wrote in his preface to the New Testament that "St. John's Gospel and his first epistle, St. Paul's epistles, especially Romans, Galatians, and Ephesians, and St. Peter's first epistle are the books that show Christ and teach you all that is necessary and salvatory for you to know, even if you were never to see or hear any other book or doctrine. Therefore St. James' epistle is really an epistle of straw, compared to these others, for it has nothing of the nature of the gospel about it."

### Its Contributions

Luther notwithstanding, James is clearly a Christian piece of writing. Full of wisdom, it is based solidly on the teachings of Jesus and is a genuine product of first-century Christianity. To be sure, it is not as directly theological as many other New Testament epistles, but then James' concern is not doctrinal (which he seems to assume) but rather ethical—how the Christian faith is to be lived on a day-by-day basis. As Johann Gottfrieds Herder wrote, "If the Epistle is of straw, then there is within that straw a very hearty, firm, nourishing ... grain" (*Briefe Zweener Brüder Jesu in unserem Kanon, in Herders sämtliche Werke,* ed. Bernard Suphan, Vol. 7, p. 500, n. 2).

### Background

James draws his language, images and ideas from three worlds: Judaism, Greek culture and early Christianity. From Christianity, he uses the language of eschatology (5:7–9), common patterns of Christian ethical instructions which parallel those of 1 Peter (1:2–4,21; 4:7–10) and echo the teachings of Jesus (e.g., 1:5,17; 2:5,8,19; 4:3; 5:12). From Judaism, he draws his insistence on the unity of God, concern for keeping the Law, and quotations from Jewish Scriptures (2:8,11,21–25; 4:6; 5:11,17–18) along with the use of certain Jewish terms (e.g., the word translated "hell" in 3:6 is the Hebrew *Gehenna*). Christianity and Judaism shared his concern for the poor and oppressed. From the Greek-speaking world—"the shared culture of the eastern Mediterranean area within the Roman Empire that resulted from the conquests of Alexander the Great" (Laws, *The Epistle of James*, p. 5)—he takes the language (which he uses with skill), the source of his Old Testament quotations (he uses the Greek Old Testament, not the Hebrew version), Greek forms of composition, and metaphors drawn from Greek and Latin sources (e.g., the horse and the ship in 3:3–4).

## Structure

Written in epistle (letter) form, James is loosely structured and rambling in style. It seems to jump from one idea to another without any overall plan, apart from that of providing a manual of Christian conduct. In fact, the book of James shares many characteristics of the sermonic style of both Greek philosophers and Jewish rabbis. As in Greek sermons, James carries on a conversation with a hypothetical opponent (2:18–26; 5:13–16), switches subjects by imperatives, relies on vivid images from everyday life (3:3–6; 5:7), illustrates points by reference to famous people (2:21–23,25; 5:11,17), uses vivid antitheses in which the right way is set alongside the wrong way (2:13,26), begins the sermon with a striking paradox that captures the hearers' attention (1:2, "Consider it pure joy … whenever you face trials"), is quite stern (2:20; 4:4), and clinches a point by means of a quotation (1:11,17; 4:6; 5:11,20) (Ropes and Barclay). It should be noted, as William Barclay writes:

> The main aim of these ancient preachers, it must be remembered, was not to investigate new truth; it was to awaken sinners to the error of their ways, and to compel them to see truths which they knew but deliberately neglected or had forgotten *(The Letters of James and Peter*, pp. 33–34).

Jewish sermons had many of the same characteristics. But rabbis also had the habit, as did James, of constructing sermons that were deliberately disconnected—a series of moral truths and exhortations, strung together like beads.

## Theme

While James clearly stands in the tradition of other Christian writers, he has some special concerns. The relationship between rich and poor crops up at various points (1:9–11; 5:1–4)—an issue of special significance to the modern affluent West. He is concerned about the use and abuse of speech (1:19,22–24,26; 2:12; 3:3–12; 5:12). He gives instruction on prayer (1:5–8; 4:2–3; 5:13–18). Above all, he is concerned with ethical behavior. How believers act, he says, has eschatological significance—future reward or punishment depends on it. In this regard, James bemoans the inconsistency of human behavior (1:6–8,22–24; 2:14–17; 4:1,3). Human beings are "double-minded" (1:8; 4:8), in sharp contrast to God, who is one (2:19).

James has been incorrectly understood by some to be contradicting Paul's doctrine of justification by faith (2:14–26). In fact, if James had Paul in mind at all, he was addressing himself to those who had perverted Paul's message—insisting that it doesn't matter what you do, as long as you have faith. James responded by asserting that works are the outward evidence of inner faith. Works make faith visible to others. In contrast, Paul was concerned with our standing before God. As is evident from Romans 12–15, Paul certainly agreed with James that faith in Christ has direct implications for how believers live.

# 1 Salutation & Trials—James 1:1–11

## THREE-PART AGENDA

**ICE-BREAKER**
15 Minutes

**BIBLE STUDY**
30 Minutes

**CARING TIME**
15–45 Minutes

***LEADER: Be sure to read pages 3–5 in the front of this book, and go over the ground rules on page 5 with the group in this first session. See page M7 in the center section for a good ice-breaker. Have your group look at pages M1–M5 in the center section and fill out the team roster on page M5.***

## TO BEGIN THE BIBLE STUDY TIME

(Choose 1 or 2)

1. How are you at taking tests? In high school or college, how much studying did you do before an exam?
2. Who is someone you turn to for wise counsel?
3. What has been one of the most joyous occasions in your life?

## READ SCRIPTURE & DISCUSS

(If you don't have time for all the questions in this section, conclude the Bible Study [30 min.] by answering question #7.)

1. What task or project have you accomplished that required great perseverance?
2. According to James, what should be a Christian's attitude when facing trials? How often is this your attitude in your own hard times?
3. Why is perseverance important? What reward comes with persevering in the faith?

***1 James, a servant of God and of the Lord Jesus Christ,***
***To the twelve tribes scattered among the nations:***

***Greetings.***

Trials and Temptations

***[2]Consider it pure joy, my brothers, whenever you face tri-***
***als of many kinds, [3]because you know that the testing of***
***your faith develops perseverance. [4]Perseverance must fin-***
***ish its work so that you may be mature and complete, not***
***lacking anything. [5]If any of you lacks wisdom, he should***
***ask God, who gives generously to all without finding fault,***
***and it will be given to him. [6]But when he asks, he must***
***believe and not doubt, because he who doubts is like a***
***wave of the sea, blown and tossed by the wind. [7]That man***
***should not think he will receive anything from the Lord; [8]he***
***is a double-minded man, unstable in all he does.***
***[9]The brother in humble circumstances ought to take***
***pride in his high position. [10]But the one who is rich should***
***take pride in his low position, because he will pass away***
***like a wild flower. [11]For the sun rises with scorching heat***
***and withers the plant; its blossom falls and its beauty is***
***destroyed. In the same way, the rich man will fade away***
***even while he goes about his business.***

4. What does it mean to be a "double-minded" person (see note on v. 8)? How can one avoid being double-minded?
5. How does James turn the assumed status of rich and poor upside down?
6. What is a trial you have faced in your life? What helped you through it?
7. What brought you to this study and what are you hoping to get out of it?

## CARING TIME

1. Have your group agree on its group covenant and ground rules (see page 5 in the front of this book).
2. Work on filling out your team roster (see page M5 in the center section). Like any winning team, every position needs to be covered.
3. Who is someone you would like to invite to this group for next week?

Share prayer requests and close in prayer. Be sure to pray for "the empty chair" (p. 4).

*P.S. At the close, pass around your books and have everyone sign the Group Directory inside the front cover.*

# Notes—James 1:1–11

**1:1** ***James.*** As discussed in the Introduction, "James" probably refers to the brother of Jesus who was known in the early church as "James the Just." The pilgrimage of James to faith is fascinating. Extra-biblical accounts tell us that James was martyred in A.D. 62. The high priest Annas the Younger seized James, who was then condemned and stoned to death. A few years later, in A.D. 66, the church in Jerusalem (which James headed) itself came to an end. Fearing the approaching Roman armies, the church members fled to Pella in the Transjordan and never returned to Jerusalem.

***a servant.*** James is so well-known that he needs no further designation. In fact, in the letter of Jude this wide recognition of James is used by the author to identify himself: "Jude, a servant of Jesus Christ and a *brother of James.*" (In contrast, it is often necessary for Paul to identify himself as an apostle, thereby asserting his apostolic authority in the matters about which he is writing.) James' modest designation of himself as "a servant" instead of "Bishop of Jerusalem" or "the brother of Jesus" is probably a reflection of his genuine humility. Here he identifies Jesus as the "Lord" (master), therefore the appropriate relationship of all others to Jesus is as servants (literally "slaves").

***the twelve tribes.*** This is a term used in the Old Testament to refer to the nation of Israel, even after 10 of the 12 tribes were lost and never reconstituted following Israel's captivity by the Assyrians. In the New Testament, it came to be associated with the Christian church. Christians saw themselves as the new Israel (Rom. 4; 9:24–26; Phil. 3:3; 1 Peter 2:9–10).

***scattered.*** The word is, literally, *diaspora* and was used by Jews to refer to those of their number living outside Palestine in the Gentile world. Here it probably refers to those Jewish Christians living outside Palestine (see 1 Peter 1:1).

**1:2–11** The three themes (testing, wisdom and riches) are connected. In order to survive the test regarding how one treats riches, wisdom from God is needed. James uses verbal echoes to link together this section. 1:1 is linked to 1:2 by the similar sound of *chairein* (greetings) and *charan* (joy). 1:2–4 are connected by the repeated word: "perseverance." Then 1:2–4 is linked to 1:5–8 by the word "lack." The word "ask" is repeated in verses 5 and 6. The word "pride" links verses 9 and 10.

**1:2** ***Consider it pure joy.*** Christians ought to view the difficulties of life with enthusiasm, because the outcome of trials will be beneficial. The joy James is talking about is not just a feeling, however. It is an active acceptance of adversity.

***my brothers.*** James is addressing his letter to those who are members of the church. This is not a letter for the world at large. The phrase "my brothers" carries with it a sense of warmth. Even though in the course of his letter James will say some very harsh things to these brothers and sisters, it is never with the sense that they are despised or even different from him (see 3:1–2). This is family! "My brothers" is a recurrent phrase in James, often used when a new subject is introduced (e.g., 1:2,19; 2:14; 3:1; 5:7).

***Christians ought to view the difficulties of life with enthusiasm, because the outcome of trials will be beneficial. The joy James is talking about is not just a feeling, however. It is an active acceptance of adversity.***

***trials of many kinds.*** The word "trials" has the dual sense of "adversity" (e.g., disease, persecution, tragedy) and "temptations" (e.g., lust, greed, trust in wealth). James is not urging Christians to seek trials. Trials will come on their own. This is simply the way life is, especially it seems, for a first-century Christian whose church is being persecuted.

**1:3** One reason that the Christian can rejoice in suffering is because immediate good does come out of the pain. In this verse James assumes that there will be good results.

***perseverance.*** Or "endurance." It is used in the sense of active overcoming, rather than passive acceptance.

**1:4** ***finish its work.*** Perfection is not automatic—it takes time and effort.

***mature and complete.*** What James has in mind here is wholeness of character. He is not calling for some sort of esoteric perfection or sinlessness. Instead, the emphasis is on moral blamelessness. He is thinking of the integrated life, in contrast to the divided person of verses 6–8.

***lacking.*** The opposite of mature and complete. This is a word used of an army that has been defeated or a person who has failed to reach a certain standard.

**1:5** ***wisdom.*** This is not just abstract knowledge, but God-given insight which leads to right living. It is the ability to make right decisions, especially about moral issues (as one must do during trials).

***generously.*** A reference both to the abundance of the gift and the spirit with which it is given. God gives fully, without hesitation and without grudging (see 2 Cor. 8:1–2).

**1:6** James now contrasts the readiness on God's part to give (v. 5) with the hesitation on people's part to ask (v. 6). Both here and in 4:3, unanswered prayer is connected to the quality of the asking, not to the unwillingness of God to give.

***believe.*** To be in *one mind* about God's ability to answer prayer, to be sure that God will hear and will act in accord with his superior wisdom. The ability to pray this sort of trusting prayer is an example of the character which is produced by trials.

**1:8** ***double-minded.*** To doubt is to be in *two minds*—to believe and to disbelieve simultaneously; to be torn between two impulses—one positive, one negative.

**1:9–11** Poverty is an example of a trial to be endured—but so too are riches, though in quite a different way. The question of riches and poverty is the third major theme in the book.

**1:9** ***humble circumstances.*** Those who are poor in a material and social sense, and who are looked down on by others because they are poor.

***take pride.*** This becomes possible when the poor see beyond immediate circumstances to their new position as children of God. They may be poor in worldly goods, but they are rich beyond imagining since they are children of God and thus heirs of the whole world. Therefore, they do in fact have a superior position in life and ought to rejoice in it.

***high position.*** In the early church, the poor gained a new sense of self-respect. Slaves found that traditional social distinctions had been obliterated (Gal. 3:28).

**1:10** ***rich.*** The peril of riches is that people come to trust in wealth as a source of security. It is a mark of double-mindedness to attempt to serve both God and money. The word "rich," in James, "always indicates one outside the community, a non-believing person. The rich, in fact, are the oppressors of the community (2:6; 5:1–6)" (Davids).

***low position.*** Jewish culture understood wealth to be a sure sign of God's favor. Here, as elsewhere (vv. 2,9), James reverses conventional expectations.

***wild flower.*** In February, Spring comes to Palestine with a blaze of color, as flowers like the lily, the poppy, and the lupine blossom along with a carpet of grass. By May, however, all the flowers and grass are brown.

**1:11** ***scorching heat.*** The hot, southeast desert wind (the sirocco) sweeps into Palestine in the Spring "like a blast of hot air when an oven door is opened" (Barclay). It blows day and night until the verdant cover is withered and brown.

***fade away.*** Wealth gives an uncertain security, since it is apt to be swept away as abruptly as desert flowers (see Isa. 40:6–8).

# 2 Trials & Temptations—James 1:12–18

## THREE-PART AGENDA

**ICE-BREAKER**
15 Minutes

**BIBLE STUDY**
30 Minutes

**CARING TIME**
15–45 Minutes

***LEADER: If there's a new person in your group in this session, start with an ice-breaker (see page M7 in the center section). Then begin the session with a word of prayer. If you have more than nine in your group, see the box about the "Subgrouping" on page 4. Count off around the group: "one, two, one, two, etc."—and have the "ones" move quickly to another room for the Bible Study.***

## TO BEGIN THE BIBLE STUDY TIME

(Choose 1 or 2)

1. Which of the following is most tempting to you: Speeding on an open highway? Spending all day shopping? Skipping work on a warm, sunny day?
2. As a kid, what's something for which you received an award or some kind of recognition?
3. What's the best gift you've received lately?

## READ SCRIPTURE & DISCUSS

(If you don't have time for all the questions in this section, conclude the Bible Study [30 min.] by answering question #7.)

1. Who is someone you know who deserves a special award for persevering under trial?
2. What reward will a person receive who "perseveres under trial" (v. 12) and loves God?

Trials and Temptations (cont.)

***[12]Blessed is the man who perseveres under trial, because when he has stood the test, he will receive the crown of life that God has promised to those who love him.***

***[13]When tempted, no one should say, "God is tempting me." For God cannot be tempted by evil, nor does he tempt anyone; [14]but each one is tempted when, by his own evil desire, he is dragged away and enticed. [15]Then, after desire has conceived, it gives birth to sin; and sin, when it is full-grown, gives birth to death.***

***[16]Don't be deceived, my dear brothers. [17]Every good and perfect gift is from above, coming down from the Father of the heavenly lights, who does not change like shifting shadows. [18]He chose to give us birth through the word of truth, that we might be a kind of firstfruits of all he created.***

3. In this passage, what do we learn about the origin of temptation?
4. What stages does temptation progress through to become "full-grown" sin?
5. What have you found helpful in dealing with temptation?
6. What good gift have you received from God for which you are thankful?
7. What trial or test are you currently facing? How can this group support you?

## CARING TIME

(Choose 1 or 2 of these questions before closing in prayer. Be sure to pray for the empty chair.)

1. Who did you invite to the group this week? Who would you like to invite to the next meeting to fill "the empty chair"?
2. If you were to describe the last week of your life in terms of weather, what was it like: Sunny and warm? Cold? Scattered Showers? Other? What is the forecast for the coming week?
3. How can the group pray for you this week?

*P.S. Add new group members to the Group Directory inside the front cover.*

# Notes—James 1:12–18

**Summary.** James now launches into the second statement of his three themes. Here the subject is trials and he expands on what he said about trials in verses 2–4. Here he adds two more pieces of information. In verse 12 he tells us that trials bring blessedness because out of them one receives the crown of life. In verses 2–4 the emphasis was on the joy of testing because it brings maturity. Then in verses 13–15 he looks at the source of failure during a trial. It is not God who is causing one to fail. Rather, it is one's own evil desire.

**1:12 *Blessed.*** Happy is the person who has withstood all the trials to the end.

***perseveres.*** In verse 3, James says that testing produces perseverance. Here he points out that such perseverance brings the reward of blessedness.

***stood the test.*** Such a person is like metal which has been purged by fire and is purified of all foreign substances.

***crown of life.*** As with Paul (Rom. 5:1–5) and Peter (1 Peter 1:6–7), James now focuses on the final result of endurance under trial: eternal life. Crowns were worn at weddings and feasts (and so signify joy); were given to the winner of an athletic competition (and so signify victory); and were worn by royalty (as befits children of God the King).

**1:13–15** Perseverance under trial is not the only option. People can fail. In these verses James examines the causes of such failure.

**1:13 *tempted.*** The focus shifts from *enduring* outward trials (v. 12) to *resisting* inner temptations.

***"God is tempting me."*** The natural tendency is to blame others for our failure. In this case, God is blamed for sending a test that was too hard to bear. That first-century Jewish Christians might reason in this fashion is probably a consequence of rabbinic teaching. Noting that human beings are double-minded and so inclined both toward good and evil, some rabbis concluded that in the same way that God was responsible for the positive side of human nature, he was also responsible for the evil side. One rabbinic saying reads: "God said, 'It repents me that I created the evil tendency in man ...!' " James stands opposed to this view. God does not put people into situations in order to test them. Such temptations arise quite naturally from life itself. James will go on to say in verse 14 that what turns a natural situation into a temptation is evil desire within a person.

***The natural tendency is to blame others for our failure.***

***God cannot be tempted by evil.*** Though it is permissible to translate the Greek phrase this way, according to Davids, the better translation is: "God ought not to be tested by evil persons." "This meaning ... fits the grammar of the passage: *gar* introduces a cogent reason (God ought not to be tested; ipso facto you should cease from doing it) and *de* introduces a somewhat different reason (*he* does not test one anyway, so you are wrong in accusing him). Furthermore, this translation shows that James is drawing upon an important theme in Jewish theology: people in tight places tend to turn and challenge God, and they ought never to do so (for it is unfaith). The theme is summed up in the deuteronomic command, 'You shall not put the Lord your God to the test, as you tested him at Massah' (Deut. 6:16)" (Davids, NIGTC).

***nor does he tempt anyone.*** God does not lure anyone into a tempting situation just to see whether that person will stand or fall. That is not God's nature. He does not desire evil nor cause evil.

**1:14–15** The steps in temptation are explained by reference to the birth process ("conceived," "birth," "full-grown"). The possibility of an evil act is entertained, then acted on again and again (the thought becomes deed) until it finally brings death. In fact, the picture here is of a seductress who entices a victim into her bed, and conceives a child whose name is *sin.* This child, in turn, produces his own offspring which is the monster called *death.* This same chain from desire to death is described by Paul in Romans 7:7–12.

**1:14 *evil desire.*** The true source of evil is a person's own inner inclination (see Mark 7:21–23).

***dragged away and enticed.*** A fishing image, "suggestive of a fish swimming in a straight course and then drawn off towards something that seems attractive, only to discover that the bait has a deadly hook in it" (Tasker).

**1:15** The opposite of "the crown of life"; the point of no-return where a repeated act has become so ingrained that we have no ability to restrain ourselves.

***God does not put people into situations in order to test them. Such temptations arise quite naturally from life itself.***

**1:16–18** Far from tempting people, God gives gifts, most notably the gift of new life.

**1:17** This is a line of Greek poetry, either original or a quotation from an unknown source.

***Father of the heavenly lights.*** God is the creator of the stars.

***shifting shadows.*** All created things, even stars, change and vary. God does not.

**1:18** ***birth.*** The contrast is made between sin which gives birth to death and the Gospel *(the word of truth)* which gives birth to life and brings into being God's children.

***firstfruits.*** At the beginning of the harvest, the earliest produce was offered to God as a symbol that the whole harvest was his.

# 3 Listening & Doing—James 1:19–27

## THREE-PART AGENDA

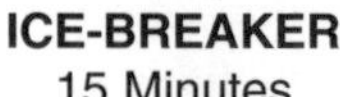

**ICE-BREAKER**
15 Minutes

**BIBLE STUDY**
30 Minutes

**CARING TIME**
15–45 Minutes

***LEADER: Remember to choose an appropriate ice-breaker if you have a new person at the meeting (see page M7 in the center section), and then begin with a prayer. If you have more than nine in your group, divide into subgroups of 4–6 for the Bible Study (see the box about the "Subgrouping" on page 4).***

## TO BEGIN THE BIBLE STUDY TIME

(Choose 1 or 2)

1. What is your biggest pet-peeve—the thing that really makes you mad?
2. What things are you sure to check in the mirror for, before leaving the house in the morning?
3. When it comes to getting angry, do you tend to have a short or long fuse?

## READ SCRIPTURE & DISCUSS

(If you don't have time for all the questions in this section, conclude the Bible Study [30 min.] by answering question #7.)

1. When was a time you wish you had been "quick to listen" and "slow to speak" (v. 19)?
2. Of the three areas in verse 19, which are you strongest in? Which one needs the most improvement?
3. What is "'the word planted in you" and how can it "save you" (v. 21)?

Listing and Doing

Listening and Doing

***19**My dear brothers, take note of this: Everyone should be quick to listen, slow to speak and slow to become angry, **20**for man's anger does not bring about the righteous life that God desires. **21**Therefore, get rid of all moral filth and the evil that is so prevalent and humbly accept the word planted in you, which can save you.*

***22**Do not merely listen to the word, and so deceive yourselves. Do what it says. **23**Anyone who listens to the word but does not do what it says is like a man who looks at his face in a mirror **24**and, after looking at himself, goes away and immediately forgets what he looks like. **25**But the man who looks intently into the perfect law that gives freedom, and continues to do this, not forgetting what he has heard, but doing it—he will be blessed in what he does.*

***26**If anyone considers himself religious and yet does not keep a tight rein on his tongue, he deceives himself and his religion is worthless. **27**Religion that God our Father accepts as pure and faultless is this: to look after orphans and widows in their distress and to keep oneself from being polluted by the world.*

4. How does the term "Sunday Christian" illustrate James' point in verses 22–24? Conversely, what does the life of someone described in verse 25 look like?
5. In what area of your life could you do a better job at applying God's Word rather than merely listening to it?
6. On a scale of 1 (thick smog) to 10 (all clear), how much exposure to the world's "pollution" did you have last week? What can you do to protect yourself in the coming week?
7. What is something this group can plan to do to demonstrate "pure and faultless" religion (v. 27) ?

## CARING TIME

(Choose 1 or 2 of these questions before closing in prayer. Be sure to pray for the empty chair.)

1. Does the group have a person for every position on the team roster (review p. M5)?
2. How is your relationship with God right now: Close? Distant? Improving? Strained? Other?
3. How can the group help you in prayer this week?

# Notes—James 1:19–27

**Summary.** In chapter one James twice introduces the three main subjects of his book. In this session he identifies for the second time, the second and third points he will discuss in his book—speech (vv. 19–21) and generosity (vv. 22–27).

**1:19–21** Having just mentioned God's Word (v. 18), James shifts here to the subject of human words. From the "word of truth" he moves to the "word of anger." James is still, in fact, focusing on the theme of wisdom, except that now his concern is with the relationship between wisdom and speech—a connection he will make plainer in 3:1–4:12. James 1:16–18 parallels this section. There he pointed out that wisdom is a gift of God. Here he points out that the wise person is slow to speak.

**1:19b** The heart of what James wants to say is found in this proverb. This is not a new teaching. The Bible often commends the value of listening and the danger of too-hasty speech.

***slow to speak.*** One needs to consider carefully what is to be said, rather than impulsively and carelessly launching into words that are not wise.

***slow to become angry.*** James does not forbid anger. Repressed anger will eventually come out and then it can be quite destructive. Also, at times, anger is the only appropriate response to a situation. However, James does caution against responding in anger at every opportunity.

**1:20** This verse is reminiscent of what Jesus said in the Sermon on the Mount (Matt. 5:21-22).

***the righteous life.*** Human anger does not produce the kind of life that God wants.

**1:21** If Christians are to speak wisely, they must prepare to do so by the dual action of ridding themselves of all that is corrupt (and not of God), and then by humbly relying upon the Word of God which is within them already.

***get rid of.*** This verb means literally, "to lay aside" or "to strip off," as one would do with filthy clothing. To be in tune with God's purpose first requires this negative action—this rejection or repentance of all that drags one down.

***all moral filth and the evil.*** The two Greek words here refer to actual dirt and are used as a metaphor for moral uncleanness. Given the context, they probably refer primarily to vulgar and malicious speech (Laws). The second word has proven very difficult to translate properly. In the King James Bible it is translated "superfluity of naughtiness." The New English Bible renders it "reckless dissipation." The Revised Standard Version translates it as "rank growth of wickedness."

***If Christians are to speak wisely, they must prepare to do so by the dual action of ridding themselves of all that is corrupt (and not of God), and then by humbly relying upon the Word of God which is within them already.***

***humbly accept.*** Having renounced evil (a negative act), the next step is to accept that which is good (a positive act). This same twofold action of repentance and faith (rejecting evil and accepting God) is the path whereby people come to Christian faith in the first place. Repentance and faith are also the key to living out the Christian life. James has already twice mentioned the idea of receiving God's gifts (vv. 5 and 17). This receiving must be done humbly. This attitude contrasts directly with anger about which he just spoke.

***the word.*** This is the same "word of truth" mentioned in verse 18. In contrast to the quick and angry words of people (words which hurt and destroy), there is the Word of God which saves.

***planted in you.*** They are Christians already. They have the life of God in them. It is now up to them to act upon what is already theirs. They must actualize in their lives the truth of God.

**1:22–27** The concept of *accepting* the Word of God (v. 21) leads James to the concept of *doing* the Word of God. Thus he moves from proper speech to proper action, which in this case is charity toward those in need. In this way he gets to his third theme, the idea that Christians are called upon to be generous in the face of poverty.

**1:22** ***merely listen.*** The Christian must not just hear the Word of God. A response is required.

***deceive yourselves.*** It does not matter how well a person may know the teaching of the apostles or how much Scripture he or she has memorized. To make mere knowledge of God's will the sole criterion for the religious life is dangerous and self-deceptive.

***Do what it says.*** This is James' main point in this section.

**1:23–24** James illustrates his point with a metaphor. The person who reads Scripture (which is a mirror to the Christian, because in it his or her true state is shown) and then goes away unchanged is like the person who gets up in the morning and sees how dirty and disheveled he or she is, but then promptly forgets about it (when the proper response would be to get cleaned up).

**1:25** In contrast is the person who not only acts to correct what is discovered to be wrong but then goes on acting in this way.

***The Christian must not just hear the Word of God. A response is required.***

***the perfect law.*** The reference is probably to the teachings of Jesus which set one free, in contradistinction to the Jewish Law which brought bondage (see Rom. 8:2).

***continues.*** Such people do not happen to notice a command and then act on it once, they make that insight a *continuing* part of their lives.

***blessed.*** The sheer act of keeping this law is a happy experience in and of itself because it produces good fruit, now and in the future.

**1:26–27** In these verses, James sums up what he has said in chapter 1 by way of introduction. He says that the mark of the true Christian is first, the ability to control the tongue (the theme of speech and wisdom); second, the willingness to engage in acts of charity (the theme of generosity in the face of poverty and wealth); and third, the attempt to overcome the trials and temptations offered by the world (the theme of testing).

**1:26** ***considers himself.*** The focus is on a person's own self-assessment of his or her religious commitment. In contrast, in verse 27, James states what God considers as truly religious.

***religious.*** The emphasis here is probably on the overt acts of religion, such as scrupulous observance of the details of worship and personal acts of piety.

***a tight reign on his tongue.*** The inability to control one's speech (as in gossip and criticism) is the mark of the person who thinks he or she is religious but really is not.

**1:27** ***Religion.*** True religion, it turns out, has more to do with acts of charity than acts of piety. It involves caring for others and avoiding the corrupting influence of one's culture.

***orphans and widows.*** In the Old Testament, orphans and widows are the poor and oppressed, whom God's people are to care for because God cares for them (Deut. 10:17–18; 24:17–22). A child without the protection and provision of parents is at the mercy of the community. So too is the widow who typically had an insecure place in ancient society. She had a certain social stigma to overcome because for a man to die before he was old was considered a judgment on his sin and this disgrace was extended to his widow. A widow also found it difficult to support herself given the social situation of the times.

***polluted.*** Unstained, pure, undefiled.

***world.*** This refers to the world system that is in opposition to God.

# 4 Favoritism Forbidden—James 2:1–13

## THREE-PART AGENDA

**ICE-BREAKER**
15 Minutes

**BIBLE STUDY**
30 Minutes

**CARING TIME**
15–45 Minutes

***LEADER: If there's a new person in this session, start with an ice-breaker from the center section (see page M7). Remember to stick closely to the three-part agenda and the time allowed for each segment. Is your group praying for the empty chair? As the leader, you may want to choose question #1 in the Caring Time to facilitate the group in handling accountability issues.***

## TO BEGIN THE BIBLE STUDY TIME

(Choose 1 or 2)

1. What is your favorite outfit to wear?
2. For what event would you buy the "best seats": The Super Bowl? A Broadway play? A concert by your favorite group? Other?
3. On what occasion have you shown up over- or under-dressed?

## READ SCRIPTURE & DISCUSS

(If you don't have time for all the questions in this section, conclude the Bible Study [30 min.] by answering question #7.)

1. When have you either been misjudged based on your appearance or misjudged someone else?
2. In general, what are some ways people show favoritism?
3. How does God look on favoritism? When has favoritism hurt you?

Favoritism Forbidden

**2** ***My brothers, as believers in our glorious Lord Jesus***
***Christ, don't show favoritism. 2Suppose a man comes***
***into your meeting wearing a gold ring and fine clothes, and***
***a poor man in shabby clothes also comes in. 3If you show***
***special attention to the man wearing fine clothes and say,***
***"Here's a good seat for you," but say to the poor man, "You***
***stand there" or "Sit on the floor by my feet," 4have you not***
***discriminated among yourselves and become judges with***
***evil thoughts?***
***5Listen, my dear brothers: Has not God chosen those***
***who are poor in the eyes of the world to be rich in faith and***
***to inherit the kingdom he promised those who love him?***
***6But you have insulted the poor. Is it not the rich who are***
***exploiting you? Are they not the ones who are dragging***
***you into court? 7Are they not the ones who are slandering***
***the noble name of him to whom you belong?***
***8If you really keep the royal law found in Scripture, "Love***
***your neighbor as yourself,"[a] you are doing right. 9But if you***
***show favoritism, you sin and are convicted by the law as***
***lawbreakers. 10For whoever keeps the whole law and yet***
***stumbles at just one point is guilty of breaking all of it. 11For***
***he who said, "Do not commit adultery,"[b] also said, "Do not***
***murder."[c] If you do not commit adultery but do commit***
***murder, you have become a lawbreaker.***
***12Speak and act as those who are going to be judged by***
***the law that gives freedom, 13because judgment without***
***mercy will be shown to anyone who has not been merciful.***
***Mercy triumphs over judgment!***

[a]8 Lev. 19:18 [b]11 Exodus 20:14; Deut. 5:18 [c]11 Exodus 20:13; Deut. 5:17

4. What is the lesson in this passage for how we are to relate to others—rich and poor?
5. Do you feel you are better at showing mercy or receiving mercy? When has someone shown mercy to you?
6. What grade would you give yourself for living by the "royal law" (v. 8)?
7. What is one practical way you can "Love your neighbor as yourself" this week?

## CARING TIME

(Choose 1 or 2 of these questions before closing in prayer. Be sure to pray for the empty chair.)

1. For what would you like this group to help hold you accountable?
2. How are you doing at inviting others to the group? Who could you invite for next week?
3. How can the group support you in prayer this week?

# Notes—James 2:1–13

**Summary.** James now begins his exposition of his first theme: poverty and generosity (2:1–26). Notice that he treats these themes in the reverse order from which he presented them in his introduction. In this chapter his focus is on the question of the rich and the poor. Christians are to have a different ethic than that of the world. They are not to favor the wealthy simply because they are wealthy, nor are they to despise the poor simply because they are poor. The poor are to be welcomed and aided. In fact, one's faith is shown by acts of generosity to the poor. The first half of the chapter (2:1–13) focuses on a warning against prejudice.

**2:1–9** James' point is quite straightforward: to discriminate between people is inconsistent with the Christian faith. This is another example of how Christian faith must be expressed in right behavior.

**2:1** James appeals to them as "believers in our glorious Lord Jesus Christ" not to discriminate. His reason is that Jesus alone is the "glorious Lord." There is only one Lord and he saves both rich and poor on the same basis—belief in him. Rich and poor are alike before their common Lord.

***glorious.*** Jesus is described here by means of a word that denotes the presence of God. When God draws near, what people experience is the light of his splendor (see Ex. 16:10; 2 Chron. 7:1–3; Ezek. 8:4; Mark 9:2–7 and Luke 2:9). James' point is that in Jesus one sees a manifestation of God's presence.

***favoritism.*** This is the act of paying special attention to someone because he or she is rich, important, famous, powerful, etc. Such discrimination (respect of persons) is condemned throughout Scripture (see Mal. 2:9; Acts 10:34–45; Rom. 2:11; Eph. 6:9; and Col. 3:25).

**2:2–4** James now gives a specific example of how deference to the rich operates in the church. The situation he describes could well have happened in the first-century church. It was one of the few institutions where traditional social barriers had been dropped. It would have been quite possible for a wealthy landowner to belong to the same Christian assembly as one of his slaves.

**2:2 *meeting.*** The word translated "meeting" is literally "synagogue."

***a gold ring.*** This is the mark of those who belonged to the equestrian order—the second level of Roman aristocracy. These noblemen were typically wealthy. Rings (in general) were a sign of wealth. The more ostentatious would fill their fingers with rings. Early Christians were urged to wear only one ring, on the little finger, bearing the image of a dove, fish, or anchor.

***fine clothes.*** These are literally "bright and shining" garments, like those worn by the angels in Acts 10:30.

***poor man.*** The word used here denotes a beggar, a person from the lowest level of society. Had this been a low-paid worker, a different Greek word would have been used.

***shabby clothes.*** In contrast to the spotless garments of the rich man, the beggar wears filthy rags, probably because this is all he owns.

**2:4** James condemns this behavior on two grounds. First, they are making distinctions between people when, in fact, Christ came to remove all such barriers (Gal. 3:28). Second, they are prejudicing their judicial decision in favor of the rich person and not listening only to the merits of the case.

**2:4–7** James attacks this kind of discrimination. All social distinctions are null and void in the church. Partiality is clearly out of place. Both rich and poor are to be received equally. Notice that the rich are not condemned here, *per se.* They are welcome in the church. What is condemned is the insult to the poor person (v. 6).

**2:5 *those who are poor.*** The New Testament is clearly on the side of the poor. In Jesus' first sermon he declared that he was called to preach the Gospel to the poor (Luke 4:18). When John the Baptist questioned whether Jesus was actually the Messiah, in response Jesus pointed to his preaching to the poor (Matt. 11:4–5). The poor are called blessed (Luke 6:20). The poor flocked to Jesus during his ministry and later into his church (1 Cor. 1:26). As William Barclay wrote: "It is not that Christ and the Church do not want the great and the rich and the wise and the mighty ... but it was the simple fact that the gospel offered so much to the poor and demanded so much from the rich, that it was the poor who were swept into the Church."

**2:6** ***But you have insulted the poor.*** The Old Testament also condemns this behavior (see Prov. 14:21).

***exploiting you.*** In a day of abject poverty the poor were often forced to borrow money at exorbitant rates of interest just to survive. The rich profited from their need.

***dragging you into court.*** This was probably over the issue of a debt. "If a creditor met a debtor on the streets, he could seize him by the neck of his robe, nearly throttling him and literally drag him to the law courts" (Barclay).

**2:7** James levels a third charge at the rich. Not only do they exploit the poor and harass them in court, they also mock the name of Jesus. This would not be unexpected since the church was largely a collection of poor people and thus would be the object of scorn by the wealthy.

***the noble name.*** The early followers of Jesus were dubbed with the name "Christians" (Acts 11:26). At baptism they formally took upon themselves the name of Christ, knowing that they might well be vilified simply for bearing that name.

**2:8** ***really keep.*** Possibly James is here countering an argument that said in treating the rich this way they were simply obeying the law of love. His point is that if they are really loving their neighbor (and not just his wealth) they would treat the poor with equal respect.

***the royal law.*** James points to what Jesus called "the most important" commandment by which he summed up all of Old Testament law. This law of love is the central moral principle by which Christians are to order their lives (see Mark 12:28–33).

**2:10–13** Favoritism is not just transgression of a single law. In fact, it makes one answerable to the whole Law. The Jews thought of law-keeping in terms of credit and debit: did your good deeds outweigh your bad? The idea of *judgment* is connected to the need for *mercy.* In fact, what James is calling for in verses 2–3 is *mercy* for the poor. Christians are not bound by rigid laws by which they will one day be judged, as Judaism taught. So the fear of future punishment is not a deterrent to behavior. Rather, it is the inner compulsion of love that motivates the Christian to right action.

**2:12** ***the law that gives freedom.*** Judaism had become encrusted with countless rules that bound people. Christians had only one principle to follow: to love others freely as Christ freely loved them (1:25; 2:8).

***Christians are to have a different ethic than that of the world. They are not to favor the wealthy simply because they are wealthy, nor are they to despise the poor simply because they are poor. The poor are to be welcomed and aided. In fact, one's faith is shown by acts of generosity to the poor.***

# 5 Faith & Deeds—James 2:14–26

## THREE-PART AGENDA

**ICE-BREAKER**
15 Minutes

**BIBLE STUDY**
30 Minutes

**CARING TIME**
15–45 Minutes

***LEADER: Check page M7 in the center section for a good ice-breaker, particularly if you have a new person at this meeting. Is your group working well together—with everyone "fielding their position" as shown on the team roster on page M5?***

## TO BEGIN THE BIBLE STUDY TIME

(Choose 1 or 2)

1. What product have you purchased that just didn't live up to its advertised claims?
2. What is your favorite charity to work with or donate to?
3. When has a stranger done something nice for you or when have you done something nice for a stranger?

## READ SCRIPTURE & DISCUSS

(If you don't have time for all the questions in this section, conclude the Bible Study [30 min.] by answering question #7.)

1. When have you struggled most financially in your life? Who helped you?
2. What kind of faith is condemned in verse 14? In what ways does this still happen today?
3. What is the relationship between faith and deeds, according to James?
4. In what way is "faith without deeds" (v. 18) dead?

Faith and Deeds

***14 What good is it, my brothers, if a man claims to have***
***faith but has no deeds? Can such faith save him?***
***15 Suppose a brother or sister is without clothes and daily***
***food. 16 If one of you says to him, "Go, I wish you well; keep***
***warm and well fed," but does nothing about his physical***
***needs, what good is it? 17 In the same way, faith by itself, if***
***it is not accompanied by action, is dead.***

***18 But someone will say, "You have faith; I have deeds."***

***Show me your faith without deeds, and I will show you***
***my faith by what I do. 19 You believe that there is one God.***
***Good! Even the demons believe that—and shudder.***

***20 You foolish man, do you want evidence that faith with-***
***out deeds is useless[a]? 21 Was not our ancestor Abraham***
***considered righteous for what he did when he offered his***
***son Isaac on the altar? 22 You see that his faith and his***
***actions were working together, and his faith was made***
***complete by what he did. 23 And the scripture was fulfilled***
***that says, "Abraham believed God, and it was credited to***
***him as righteousness,"[b] and he was called God's friend.***
***24 You see that a person is justified by what he does and not***
***by faith alone.***

***25 In the same way, was not even Rahab the prostitute con-***
***sidered righteous for what she did when she gave lodging***
***to the spies and sent them off in a different direction? 26 As***
***the body without the spirit is dead, so faith without deeds***
***is dead.***

[a]20 Some early manuscripts *dead* [b]23 Gen. 15:6

5. What are the lessons from Abraham's and Rahab's examples? When has your faith been put to the test?
6. In what way should the lifestyle of a Christian verify their faith?
7. In what practical way can you put your faith into action this week?

## CARING TIME

(Choose 1 or 2 of these questions before closing in prayer. Be sure to pray for the empty chair.)

1. What is something for which you are particularly thankful?
2. How is the group doing with its "team assignments" (review the team roster on p. M5)?
3. How can the group remember you in prayer this week?

# Notes—James 2:14–26

**Summary.** This is part two of James' discussion of the poor. In part one (2:1–13) the issue was discrimination against the poor. Here the issue is charity toward the poor. This section parallels the previous section structurally. Both sections begin with a key assertion which is then illustrated. This is followed by a logical argument which demonstrates the point. The section is then concluded by two arguments drawn from the Bible.

**2:14 *my brothers.*** By this phrase James signals the start of a new point.

> ***Faith is invisible without deeds. If faith does not make itself known in one's lifestyle, then it is nonexistent. Deeds are the only demonstration of inner faith.***

***faith.*** James uses this word in a special way. The faith he speaks of here is mere intellectual affirmation. Such a mind-oriented profession stands in sharp contrast to the comprehensive, whole-life commitment that characterizes true New Testament faith. New Testament faith involves believing with all one's being: mind, emotions, body (behavior) and spirit. The people James has in mind differ from their pagan and Jewish neighbors only in what they profess to believe. They are orthodox Christians who believe in Jesus; however, they live no differently than anyone else.

***deeds.*** Just as James uses the word "faith" in his own way, so too he uses *deeds* (or "works"). For James, deeds have to do with proper ethical behavior. In contrast, Paul seldom calls such behavior "works." In fact, he generally avoids the word altogether and when he does use it, he equates it to the Law, i.e., "works of the Law" which clearly is not what the Christian life is all about.

***Can such faith save him?*** The implied answer to this rhetorical question is "No." This answer is based on what James just said in 2:12–13. Intellectual faith cannot save one from judgment when one has not been merciful.

**2:15 *Suppose.*** A test case is proposed through which the absurdity of claiming "faith" without corresponding "action" is made evident. Though this is a hypothetical situation it would not have been uncommon in Jerusalem for a person to lack the basics of life given the famine and the marginal economy of the area.

***a brother or sister.*** James picks an example in which the right action is absolutely clear. The person in need is a Christian from their own fellowship, not an outsider or a person far away about whom their responsibility might not be as unequivocal.

***clothes and daily food.*** Both are absolutely necessary to sustain life. A person without food and without warmth will die. The reference to clothes can be either to the outer tunic which was worn in public and which served as a blanket, or it can refer to clothes so ragged that they are of little use. This word can also be translated as "naked," having no clothes at all (as in Mark 14:51–52).

**2:16** The implication is that the Christian to whom this appeal has been made could meet the need but chooses not to, and instead offers pious platitudes.

**2:17** James did not dream up his conclusion here. It is what is taught consistently throughout the New Testament. John the Baptist taught it (Luke 3:8). Jesus taught it (Matt. 5:16; 7:15–21). And Paul taught it (Rom. 2:6; 14:12; 1 Cor. 3:8; 2 Cor. 5:10).

***dead.*** James is saying: "Your faith is not real, it is a sham. You are playing at being a Christian."

**2:18 *But someone will say.*** James responds to an imaginary critic who raises a new issue. This person contends that both faith and deeds are good on their own. "Some have faith. Others perform deeds. Both are praiseworthy. In either case, a person is religious." James disagrees that faith and deeds are unconnected. It is not a matter of either/or. It is both/and, as he shows in verse 22.

***Show me your faith without deeds.*** James replies that faith is invisible without deeds. If faith does not make itself known in one's lifestyle, then it is nonexistent. Deeds are the only demonstration of inner faith.

**2:19** James continues to press his argument. These people say they believe so he begins with the *Shema*, the central belief of both Jew and Christian: "Hear, O Israel: The LORD our God, the LORD is one" (see Deut. 6:4–5 and Mark 12:28–34). But then he goes on to point out that even the demons believe this (see Mark 1:23–24; 5:1–7; and Acts 16:16–18). And they respond with a shudder because they know that God is more powerful than they and that they are in rebellion against God. Belief in one God does not automatically lead to godly action. Orthodox faith alone—which the demons have—is not enough without an obedient lifestyle.

***shudder.*** In certain ancient documents, this word is used in connection with magic and describes the effect a sorcerer seeks from his incantations.

**2:20** ***You foolish man.*** The NIV blunts the harshness of James' language here. "You fool," he is saying. "You empty man," is the literal rendering of this phrase. This was not an uncommon way for first-century preachers to address their listeners, especially when they were using the so-called diatribe style of speaking or writing. Even Jesus used this sort of strong language (see Matt. 23:17).

**2:21–25** James concludes by offering via two illustrations from the Old Testament the evidence demanded by the fool in verse 20 for the assertion that faith is useless without deeds. In both cases faith is demonstrated by means of concrete action. Abraham actually had the knife raised over his beloved son Isaac, and Rahab actually hid the spies. Without faith, Abraham would never have even considered sacrificing his only son, nor would Rahab have defied her king at great personal risk.

**2:22** The heart of James' argument: faith and deeds working together characterize the life of the person who is truly religious. "There is a mutuality: Faith informs and motivates action; action matures faith. James is not rejecting one for the other but is instead insisting that the two are totally inseparable" (Davids, GNC).

***actions.*** This is plural because Abraham's action with Isaac was not an isolated instance, but the culmination of many actions based on faith in God.

***made complete.*** The idea is not that faith is somehow perfected by deeds. Rather, faith is brought to new maturity by such actions.

**2:23–24** Paul uses this same verse (Gen. 15:6) to demonstrate the *opposite* point in Romans 4, namely that it was not by his deed but by his faith that Abraham was justified. But, in fact, Paul and James use this verse in quite different ways. Paul's point is that Abraham believed God and was declared righteous *prior* to the ritual action (the deed) of circumcision. But James focuses on the offering up of Isaac (Gen. 22:2,9–10)—not on the act of circumcision—and declares that this act of offering up his son demonstrated that Abraham had faith. Furthermore, the works Paul has in mind are acts of ritual law-keeping such as circumcision, food laws, and the like; whereas for James it is acts of charity that he is concerned about, not fulfillment of the Law.

**2:24** ***by faith alone.*** For James faith means " 'by intellectual belief that God is one' or 'that Jesus is Lord,' whereas faith for Paul means personal commitment to Christ that leads inevitably to obedience because one is convinced that Jesus is Lord. ... James' point is that God will not approve a person just because he or she is very orthodox or can pass a test in systematic theology. He will declare someone righteous only if this faith is such that the person acts on it and produces the natural result of commitment, obedient action" (Davids, GNC).

**2:25** ***Rahab.*** Joshua sent two spies into Jericho. Their presence was detected but Rahab hid them, sent the king's soldiers off on a wild-goose chase, and then let the spies safely down the city wall (Josh. 2:1–21). Later legend says that she became a Jewish convert, married Joshua, and from her line came many priests and prophets including Ezekiel and Jeremiah.

# 6 Taming the Tongue—James 3:1–12

## THREE-PART AGENDA

**ICE-BREAKER**
15 Minutes

**BIBLE STUDY**
30 Minutes

**CARING TIME**
15–45 Minutes

***LEADER: Check page M7 in the center section for a good ice-breaker, particularly if you have a new person at this meeting. In the Caring Time, is everyone sharing and are prayer requests being followed up?***

## TO BEGIN THE BIBLE STUDY TIME

(Choose 1 or 2)

1. Growing up, who was your favorite teacher?
2. When was your first experience of riding a horse?
3. What radio, TV or newspaper personality do you appreciate for their uplifting words? Who don't you appreciate?

## READ SCRIPTURE & DISCUSS

(If you don't have time for all the questions in this section, conclude the Bible Study [30 min.] by answering question #7.)

1. When is a time you *really* put your foot in your mouth?
2. Why is it such a great responsibility to be a teacher, especially of the Scripture?
3. What do the examples of the bit, rudder and fire teach about the importance of watching what we say?
4. In light of verse 8, what hope do we have in relation to controlling our tongues?
5. What does verse 9 say about the caution and the reverence with which we should choose our words when speaking of, or to, others?

Taming the Tongue

***3** Not many of you should presume to be teachers, my brothers, because you know that we who teach will be judged more strictly. [2]We all stumble in many ways. If anyone is never at fault in what he says, he is a perfect man, able to keep his whole body in check.*

*[3]When we put bits into the mouths of horses to make them obey us, we can turn the whole animal. [4]Or take ships as an example. Although they are so large and are driven by strong winds, they are steered by a very small rudder wherever the pilot wants to go. [5]Likewise the tongue is a small part of the body, but it makes great boasts. Consider what a great forest is set on fire by a small spark. [6]The tongue also is a fire, a world of evil among the parts of the body. It corrupts the whole person, sets the whole course of his life on fire, and is itself set on fire by hell.*

*[7]All kinds of animals, birds, reptiles and creatures of the sea are being tamed and have been tamed by man, [8]but no man can tame the tongue. It is a restless evil, full of deadly poison.*

*[9]With the tongue we praise our Lord and Father, and with it we curse men, who have been made in God's likeness. [10]Out of the same mouth come praise and cursing. My brothers, this should not be. [11]Can both fresh water and salt[a] water flow from the same spring? [12]My brothers, can a fig tree bear olives, or a grapevine bear figs? Neither can a salt spring produce fresh water.*

[a]11 Greek *bitter* (see also verse 14)

6. In what ways can we make sure that what we say is pleasing to God and uplifting to others?

7. This past week, did you feel your speech was encouraging to those around you? Who do you need to encourage in the coming week?

## CARING TIME

(Choose 1 or 2 of these questions before closing in prayer. Be sure to pray for the empty chair.)

1. Congratulations! You are halfway through this study. What do you look forward to when you come to this group?

2. It's not too late to have someone new come to this group. Who can you invite for next week?

3. How would you like the group to pray for you this week?

# Notes—James 3:1–12

**Summary.** James now shifts to his second subject: wisdom. This discussion will extend from 3:1 to 4:12. In this first section, he examines the connection between speech and wisdom. In particular, he focuses on the tongue, that organ by which we produce words, the vehicles of wisdom. Words, he says, are not insignificant. Words can be wise but they can also be deadly. The tongue is such a small organ, yet it has great power. It can control the very direction of one's life. Mature people are known by their ability to control the tongue. Certain teachers were using their tongues to criticize others (and were probably being criticized in return).

**3:1 *Not many of you should presume to be teachers.*** In the early church a person did not become a teacher by going to seminary or Bible school. None existed. Instead, teachers were called and empowered by the Holy Spirit (see Rom. 12:6–7; 1 Cor. 12:28; and Eph. 4:11–13). The problem was that the gift of teaching could be imitated. It was a prestigious position and if a person were eloquent, he or she might pretend to be a teacher. False teachers were a real problem in the first century (see 1 Tim. 1:7; Titus 1:11; and 2 Peter 2:1–3).

***teachers.*** Following in the tradition of the rabbis, early Christian teachers were responsible for the moral and spiritual instruction of a local congregation. This was an especially important task in the first century since many of the Christians, being poor, would not have been very well-educated. Nor could they read or write. In contrast to apostles whose ministry was itinerant, teachers stayed in one location and taught a particular congregation. Teachers were held in great honor, but herein lay great danger. They might become puffed up with spiritual and intellectual pride (see Matt. 23:2–7). They might begin to teach their own opinions instead of God's truth. (The Judaizers did this when they started teaching that before people could become Christians, they first had to become Jews and be circumcised—see Acts 15:1–29). Or teachers might turn out to be hypocrites—teaching one thing but living another (see Rom. 2:17–24).

***judged more strictly.*** It is dangerous to fake the gift of teaching (see Matt. 12:36; 23:1–33; Mark 12:40). To mislead God's people by false words or an inappropriate lifestyle can cause great harm to those seeking to know God and follow his ways.

**3:2 *stumble.*** This word means "to trip, to slip up or to make a mistake." This is not deliberate, premeditated wrongdoing. Rather, it is failure due to inadequacy. This is a problem of faulty *reactions,* not evil *actions.*

***what he says.*** James' focus is on words, the stock-in-trade of teachers. Thus, James launches into the main theme of this section: the sins of the tongue. It is important to notice that James is not calling here for silence, only for control (see 1:19).

***Words can be wise but they can also be deadly. The tongue is such a small organ, yet it has great power. It can control the very direction of one's life. Mature people are known by their ability to control the tongue.***

***perfect.*** This same word is also used in 1:4 and in 1:25. In all three instances, it is used to describe that which is mature, complete and whole. James is not teaching that Christians should be morally perfect, living in a state of sinlessness. This is obviously impossible.

**3:3–4** As a small piece of metal directs a horse or a small rudder directs a ship, so the tongue directs the course of one's character.

**3:3 *horses.*** These huge, powerful animals can be controlled and guided by the human rider simply by means of a small bit.

**3:4 *ships.*** Ships were among the largest man-made objects that first-century people would have seen. That such a big structure driven by such powerful forces ("strong winds") could be controlled by so small a device as a rudder amply illustrates what James wants to say about the tongue. The person who controls the bit or rudder (or tongue) has control over the horse or ship (or the body).

**3:5 *fire.*** During the dry season in Palestine, the scrub brush was apt to ignite easily and spread out

SERENDIPITY

201

Game Plan

# Leadership Training Supplement

YOU ARE HERE

BIRTH

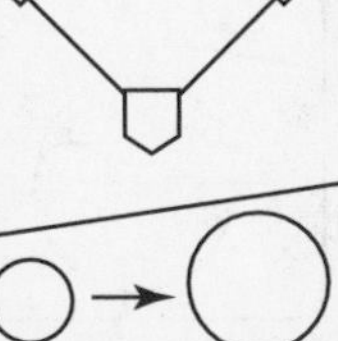

GROWTH

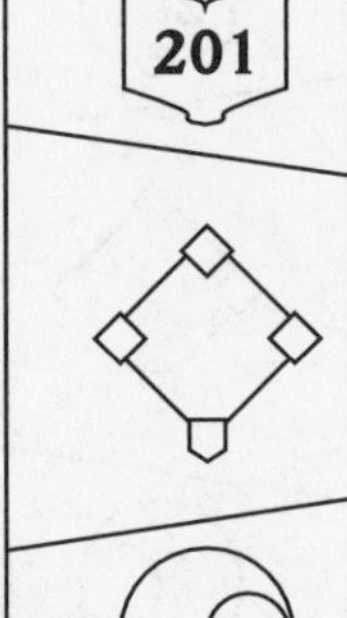


DEVELOP

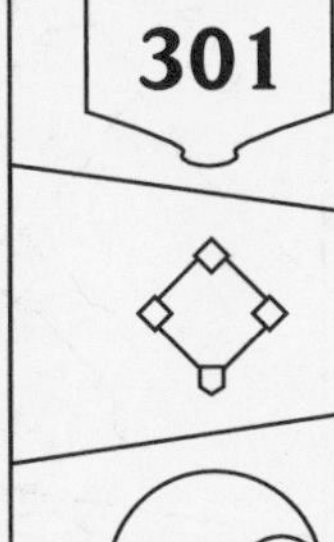


REBIRTH

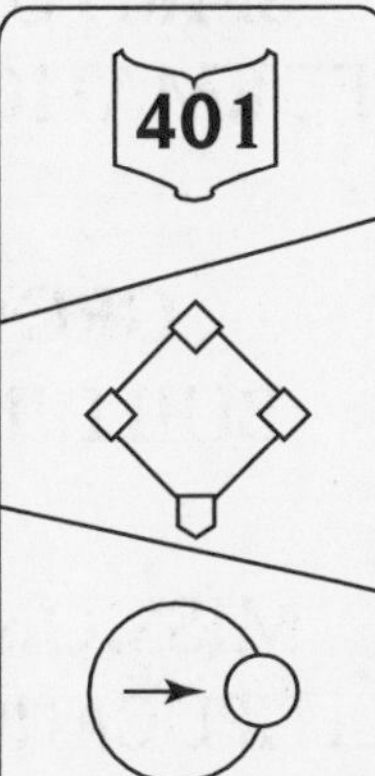

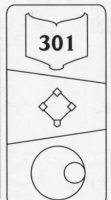

# What is the game plan for your group in the 201 stage?

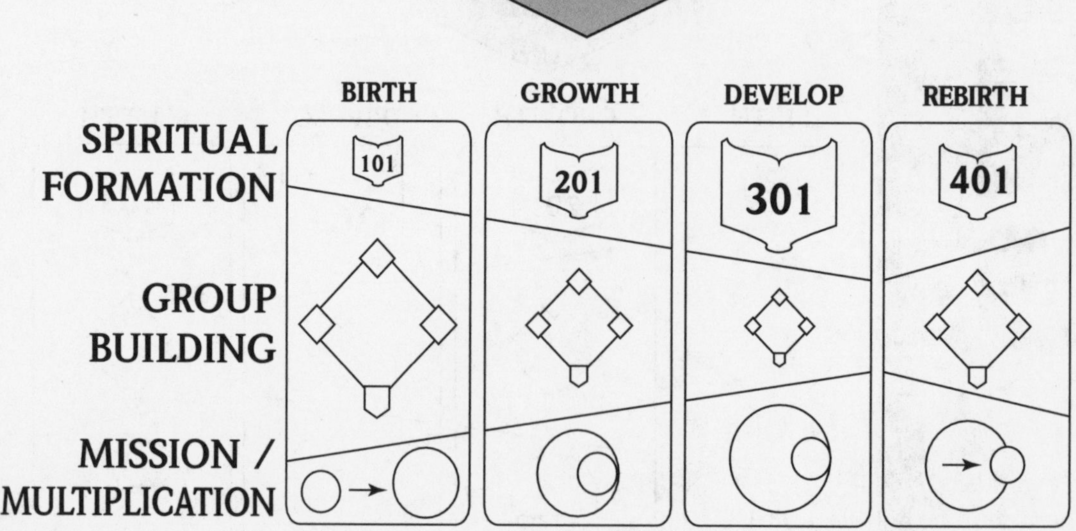

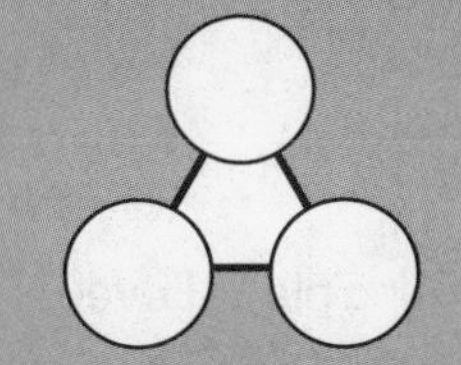

The 3-Legged Stool

The three essentials in a healthy small group are Bible Study, Group Building and Mission / Multiplication. You need all three to stay balanced—like a 3-legged stool.

- To focus only on Bible Study will lead to scholasticism.
- To focus only on Group Building will lead to narcissism.
- To focus only on Mission will lead to burnout.

You need a game plan for the life cycle of the group where all of these elements are present in a purpose-driven strategy:

# Spiritual Formation (Bible Study)

**To dig into Scripture as a group.**

Group Bible Study is quite different from individual Bible Study. The guided discussion questions are open-ended. And for those with little Bible background, there are reference notes to bring their knowledge level up so they do not feel intimidated. This helps level the playing field.

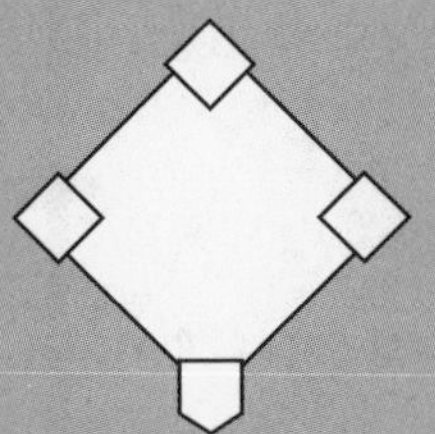

# Group Building

**To transform your group into a mission-driven team.**

The nine basic needs of a group will be assigned to nine different people. Everyone has a job to fill, and when everyone is doing their job the group will grow spiritually and numerically. When new people enter the group, there is a selection of ICE-BREAKERS to start off the meeting and let the new people get acquainted.

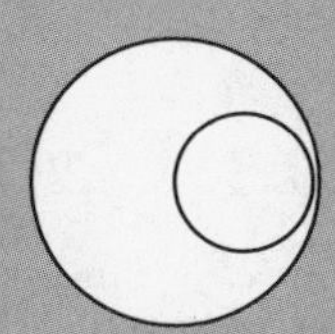

# Mission / Multiplication

**To identify the Apprentice / Leader for birthing a new group.**

In this stage, you will start dreaming about the possibility of starting a new group down the road. The questions at the close of each session will lead you carefully through the dreaming process—to help you discover an Apprentice / Leader who will eventually be the leader of a new group. This is an exciting challenge! (See page M6 for more about Mission / Multiplication.)

# Bible Study

**What is unique about Serendipity Group Bible Study?**

Bible Study for groups is based on six principles. Principle 1: Level the playing field so that everyone can share—those who know the Bible and those who do not know the Bible. Principle 2: Share your spiritual story and let the people in your group get to know you. Principle 3: Ask open-ended questions that have no right or wrong answers. Principle 4: Use the 3-part agenda. Principle 5: Subdivide into smaller subgroups so that everyone can participate. Principle 6: Affirm One Another—"Thanks for sharing."

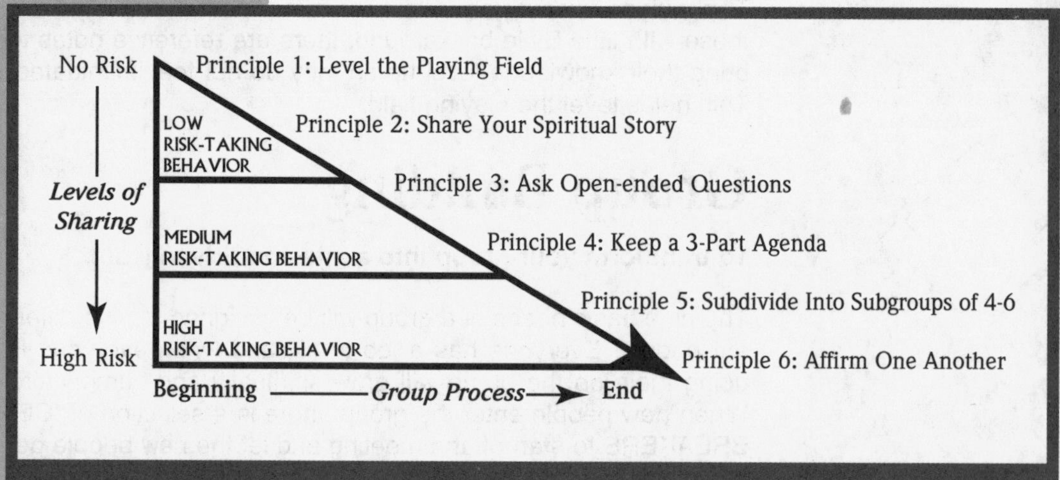

# Group Building

**What are the jobs that are needed on your team roster?**

In the first or second session of this course, you need to fill out the roster on the next page. Then check every few weeks to see that everyone is "playing their position." If you do not have nine people in your group, you can double up on jobs until new people join your group and are assigned a job. The goal is to field a team. Building a team will better prepare you to rebirth a new group when the group becomes pregnant.

# Your Small Group Team Roster

**Mission Leader**
(Left Field)
Keeps group focused on the mission to invite new people and eventually give birth to a new group. This person needs to be passionate and have a long-term perspective.

______________________

**Host**
(Center Field)
Environmental engineer in charge of meeting location. Always on the lookout for moving to a new meeting location where new people will feel the "home field advantage."

______________________

**Party Leader**
(Right Field)
Designates who is going to bring refreshments. Plans a party every month or so where new people are invited to visit and children are welcome.

______________________

**Caretaker**
(Shortstop)
Takes new members under their wing. Makes sure they get acquainted. Always has an extra book, name tags and a list of group members and phone numbers.

______________________

**Bible Study Leader**
(Second Base)
Takes over in the Bible Study time (30 minutes). Follows the agenda. Keeps the group moving. This person must be very time-conscious.

______________________

**Group Leader**
(Pitcher)
Puts ball in play. Team encourager. Motivator. Sees to it that everyone is involved in the team effort.

______________________

**Worship Leader**
(First Base)
Leads the group in singing and prayer when it is appropriate. Also leads the icebreaker to get acquainted, before the opening prayer.

______________________

**Caring Time Leader**
(Third Base)
Takes over in the Caring Time. Records prayer requests and follows up on any prayer needs during the week. This person is the "heart" of the group.

______________________

**Apprentice / Leader**
(Catcher)
The other half of the battery. Observes the infield. Calls "time" to discuss strategy and regroup. Stays focused.

______________________

# Mission / Multiplication

**Where are you in the 4-stage life cycle of your mission?**

You can't sit on a one-legged stool—or even a two-legged stool. It takes all three. The same is true of a small group; you need all three legs. A Bible Study and Care Group will eventually fall if it does not have a mission.

The mission goal is to eventually give birth to a new group. In this 201 course, the goals are: 1) to keep inviting new people to join your group and 2) to discover the Apprentice / Leader and leadership core for starting a new group down the road.

When a new person comes to the group, start off the meeting with one of the ice-breakers on the following pages. These ice-breakers are designed to be fun and easy to share, but they have a very important purpose—that is, to let the new person get acquainted with the group and share their spiritual story with the group, and hear the spiritual stories of those in the group.

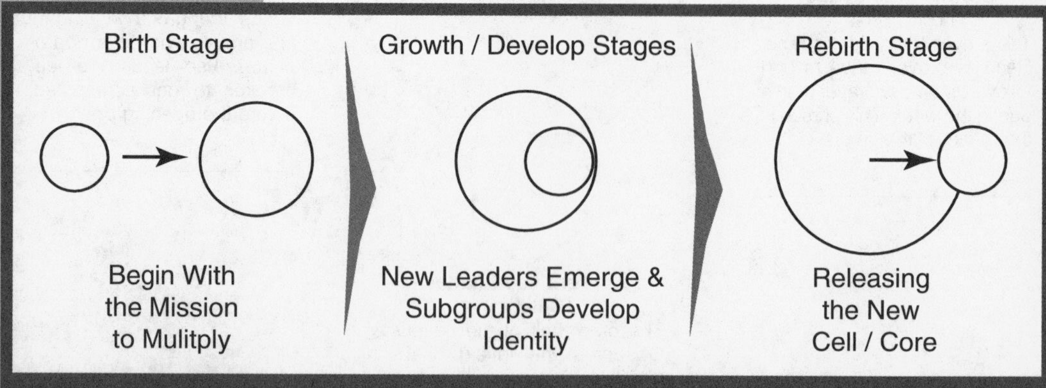

# Ice-Breakers

## Get Acquainted / New People

**Session 1** or when a new person comes to a meeting


I Am Somebody Who ... M8
Press Conference M8
Down Memory Lane M9
Wallet Scavenger Hunt M9
The Grand Total M10
Find Yourself in the Picture M11
Four Facts, One Lie M11
Old-Fashioned Auction M12
Places in My Life M13
The Four Quaker Questions M13
KWIZ Show M14


## To Report In to Your Group

**Middle Sessions**


Let Me Tell You About My Day M16
Music in My Life M17
My Childhood Table M17
Home Improvement M18
How Is It With Your Soul? M18
My Spiritual Journey M19
Bragging Rights M19
Personal Habits M20
American Graffiti M20


## To Affirm and Assign Roles

**Latter Sessions**


Group Orchestra M21
Broadway Show M22
Wild Predictions M23
Career Placements M24
You and Me, Partner M25
My Gourmet Group M26


## To Evaluate and Say Good-bye

**Last Session**


Thank You M27
Academy Awards M28
You Remind Me of Jesus M29
Reflections M30
Human Bingo / Party Mixer M31
Group Covenant M32

# I Am Somebody Who ...

Rotate around the group, one person reading the first item, the next person reading the second item, etc. Before answering, let everyone in the group try to GUESS what the answer would be: "Yes" ... "No" ... or "Maybe." After everyone has guessed, explain the answer. Anyone who guessed right gets $10. When every item on the list has been read, the person with the most "money" WINS.

I AM SOMEBODY WHO ...

**Y N M**

❐ ❐ ❐ would go on a blind date
❐ ❐ ❐ sings in the shower
❐ ❐ ❐ listens to music full blast
❐ ❐ ❐ likes to dance
❐ ❐ ❐ cries at movies
❐ ❐ ❐ stops to smell the flowers
❐ ❐ ❐ daydreams a lot
❐ ❐ ❐ likes to play practical jokes
❐ ❐ ❐ makes a "to do" list
❐ ❐ ❐ loves liver
❐ ❐ ❐ won't use a portable toilet
❐ ❐ ❐ likes thunderstorms
❐ ❐ ❐ enjoys romance novels
❐ ❐ ❐ loves crossword puzzles
❐ ❐ ❐ hates flying
❐ ❐ ❐ fixes my own car

**Y N M**

❐ ❐ ❐ would enjoy skydiving
❐ ❐ ❐ has a black belt in karate
❐ ❐ ❐ watches soap operas
❐ ❐ ❐ is afraid of the dark
❐ ❐ ❐ goes to bed early
❐ ❐ ❐ plays the guitar
❐ ❐ ❐ talks to plants
❐ ❐ ❐ will ask a stranger for directions
❐ ❐ ❐ sleeps until the last second
❐ ❐ ❐ likes to travel alone
❐ ❐ ❐ reads the financial page
❐ ❐ ❐ saves for a rainy day
❐ ❐ ❐ lies about my age
❐ ❐ ❐ yells at the umpire
❐ ❐ ❐ closes my eyes during scary movies

# Press Conference

This is a great activity for a new group or when new people are joining an established group. Interview one person with these questions.

1. What is your nickname and how did you get it?
2. Where did you grow up? Where was the "watering hole" in your hometown—where kids got together?
3. What did you do for kicks then? What about now?
4. What was the turning point in your spiritual life?
5. What prompted you to come to this group?
6. What do you want to get out of this group?

## Down Memory Lane

Celebrate the childhood memories of the way you were. Choose one or more of the topics listed below and take turns answering the question related to it. If time allows, do another round.

HOME SWEET HOME–What do you remember about your childhood home?

TELEVISION—What was your favorite TV program or radio show?

OLD SCHOOLHOUSE—What were your best and worst subjects in school?

LIBRARY—What did you like to read (and where)?

TELEPHONE—How much time did you spend on the phone each day?

MOVIES—Who was your favorite movie star?

CASH FLOW—What did you do for spending money?

SPORTS—What was your favorite sport or team?

GRANDPA'S HOUSE—Where did your grandparents live? When did you visit them?

POLICE—Did you ever get in trouble with the law?

WEEKENDS—What was the thing to do on Saturday night?

## Wallet Scavenger Hunt

With your wallet or purse, use the set of questions below. You get two minutes in silence to go through your possessions and find these items. Then break the silence and "show-and-tell" what you have chosen. For instance, "The thing I have had for the longest time is ... this picture of me when I was a baby."

1. The thing I have had for the LONGEST TIME in my wallet is ...

2. The thing that has SENTIMENTAL VALUE is ...

3. The thing that reminds me of a FUN TIME is ...

4. The most REVEALING thing about me in my wallet is ...

# The Grand Total

This is a fun ice-breaker that has additional uses. You can use this ice-breaker to divide your group into two subgroups (odds and evens). You can also calculate who has the highest and lowest totals if you need a fun way to select someone to do a particular task, such as bring refreshments or be first to tell their story.

Fill each box with the correct number and then total your score. When everyone is finished, go around the group and explain how you got your total.

| | | | | |
|---|---|---|---|---|
| Number of hours you sleep | x | Number of miles you walk daily | = | Subtotal |
| Number of speeding tickets you've received | – | Number of times sent to principal's office | = | Subtotal |
| Number of hours spent watching TV daily | ÷ | Number of books you read this year for fun | = | Subtotal |
| Number of push-ups you can do | + | Number of pounds you lost this year | = | Subtotal |
| | | | | GRAND TOTAL |

# Find Yourself in the Picture

In this drawing, which child do you identify with—or which one best portrays you right now? Share with your group which child you would choose and why. You can also use this as an affirmation exercise, by assigning each person in your group to a child in the picture.

# Four Facts, One Lie

Everyone in the group should answer the following five questions. One of the five answers should be a lie! The rest of the group members can guess which of your answers is a lie.

1. At age 7, my favorite TV show was ...
2. At age 9, my hero was ...
3. At age 11, I wanted to be a ...
4. At age 13, my favorite music was ...
5. Right now, my favorite pastime is ...

# Old-Fashioned Auction

Just like an old-fashioned auction, conduct an out loud auction in your group—starting each item at $50. Everybody starts out with $1,000. Select an auctioneer. This person can also get in on the bidding. Remember, start the bidding on each item at $50. Then, write the winning bid in the left column and the winner's name in the right column. Remember, you only have $1,000 to spend for the whole game. AUCTIONEER: Start off by asking, "Who will give me $50 for a 1965 red MG convertible?" ... and keep going until you have a winner. Keep this auction to 10 minutes.

| WINNING BID | | WINNER |
|---|---|---|
| $__________ | 1965 red MG convertible in perfect condition | __________ |
| $__________ | Winter vacation in Hawaii for two | __________ |
| $__________ | Two Super Bowl tickets on the 50-yard line | __________ |
| $__________ | One year of no hassles with my kids / parents | __________ |
| $__________ | Holy Land tour hosted by my favorite Christian leader | __________ |
| $__________ | Season pass to ski resort of my choice | __________ |
| $__________ | Two months off to do anything I want, with pay | __________ |
| $__________ | Home theater with surround sound | __________ |
| $__________ | Breakfast in bed for one year | __________ |
| $__________ | Two front-row tickets at the concert of my choice | __________ |
| $__________ | Two-week Caribbean cruise with my spouse in honeymoon suite | __________ |
| $__________ | Shopping spree at Saks Fifth Avenue | __________ |
| $__________ | Six months of maid service | __________ |
| $__________ | All-expense-paid family vacation to Disney World | __________ |

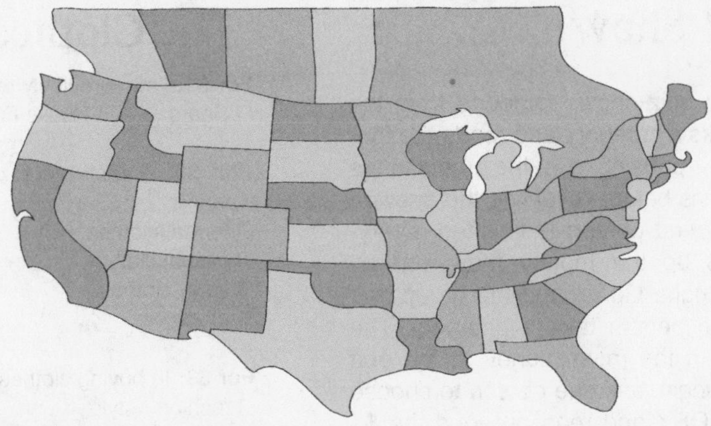

# Places in My Life

On the map above, put six dots to indicate these significant places in your journey. Then go around and have each person explain the dots:

- the place where I was born
- the place where I spent most of my life
- the place where I first fell in love
- the place where I went or would like to go on a vacation
- the place where God first became real to me
- the place where I would like to retire

# The Four Quaker Questions

This is an old Quaker activity which Serendipity has adapted over the years. Go around the group and share your answers to the questions, everyone answering #1. Then, everyone answers #2, etc. This ice-breaker has been known to take between 30 and 60 minutes for some groups.

1. Where were you living between the ages of 7 and 12, and what were the winters like then?

2. How was your home heated during that time?

3. What was the center of warmth in your life when you were a child? (It could be a place in the house, a time of year, a person, etc.)

4. When did God become a "warm" person to you ... and how did it happen?

# KWIZ Show

Like a TV quiz show, someone from the group picks a category and reads the four questions—pausing to let the others in the group guess before revealing the answer. When the first person is finished, everyone adds up the money they won by guessing right. Go around the group and have each person take a category. The person with the most money at the end wins. To begin, ask one person to choose a CATEGORY and read out loud the $1 question. Before answering, let everyone try to GUESS the answer. When everyone has guessed, the person answers the question, and anyone who guessed right puts $1 in the margin, etc. until the first person has read all four questions in the CATEGORY.

## Clothes

**For $1:** I'm more likely to shop at:
❒ Sears ❒ Saks Fifth Avenue

**For $2:** I feel more comfortable wearing:
❒ formal clothes
❒ casual clothes
❒ sport clothes
❒ grubbies

**For $3:** In buying clothes, I look for:
❒ fashion / style
❒ price
❒ name brand
❒ quality

**For $4:** In buying clothes, I usually:
❒ shop all day for a bargain
❒ go to one store, but try on everything
❒ buy the first thing I try on
❒ buy without trying it on

## Tastes

**For $1:** In music, I am closer to:
❒ Bach ❒ Beatles

**For $2:** In furniture, I prefer:
❒ Early American
❒ French Provincial
❒ Scandinavian—contemporary
❒ Hodgepodge—little of everything

**For $3:** My favorite choice of reading material is:
❒ science fiction ❒ sports
❒ mystery ❒ romance

**For $4:** If I had $1,000 to splurge, I would buy:
❒ one original painting
❒ two numbered prints
❒ three reproductions and an easy chair
❒ four cheap imitations, an easy chair and a color TV

## Travel

**For $1:** For travel, I prefer:
❒ excitement ❒ enrichment

**For $2:** On a vacation, my lifestyle is:
❒ go-go all the time
❒ slow and easy
❒ party every night and sleep in

**For $3:** In packing for a trip, I include:
❒ toothbrush and change of underwear
❒ light bag and good book
❒ small suitcase and nice outfit
❒ all but the kitchen sink

**For $4:** If I had money to blow, I would choose:
❒ one glorious night in a luxury hotel
❒ a weekend in a nice hotel
❒ a full week in a cheap motel
❒ two weeks camping in the boondocks

# Habits

**For $1:** I am more likely to squeeze the toothpaste:
❐ in the middle ❐ from the end

**For $2:** If I am lost, I will probably:
❐ stop and ask directions
❐ check the map
❐ find the way by driving around

**For $3:** I read the newspaper starting with the:
❐ front page
❐ funnies
❐ sports
❐ entertainment section

**For $4:** When I get ready for bed, I put my clothes:
❐ on a hanger in the closet
❐ folded neatly over a chair
❐ into a hamper or clothes basket
❐ on the floor

# Food

**For $1:** I prefer to eat at a:
❐ fast-food restaurant
❐ fancy restaurant

**For $2:** On the menu, I look for something:
❐ familiar
❐ different
❐ way-out

**For $3:** When eating chicken, my preference is a:
❐ drumstick
❐ wing
❐ breast
❐ gizzard

**For $4:** I draw the line when it comes to eating:
❐ frog legs
❐ snails
❐ raw oysters
❐ Rocky Mountain oysters

# Shows

**For $1:** I am more likely to:
❐ go see a first-run movie
❐ rent a video at home

**For $2:** On TV, my first choice is:
❐ news
❐ sports
❐ sitcoms

**For $3:** If a show gets too scary, I will usually:
❐ go to the restroom
❐ close my eyes
❐ clutch a friend
❐ love it

**For $4:** In movies, I prefer:
❐ romantic comedies
❐ serious drama
❐ action films
❐ Disney animation

# Work

**For $1:** I prefer to work at a job that is:
❐ too big to handle
❐ too small to be challenging

**For $2:** The job I find most unpleasant to do is:
❐ cleaning the house
❐ working in the yard
❐ balancing the checkbook

**For $3:** In choosing a job, I look for:
❐ salary
❐ security
❐ fulfillment
❐ working conditions

**For $4:** If I had to choose between these jobs, I would choose:
❐ pickle inspector at processing plant
❐ complaint officer at department store
❐ bedpan changer at hospital
❐ personnel manager in charge of firing

# Let Me Tell You About My Day

What was your day like today? Use one of the characters below to help you describe your day to the group. Feel free to elaborate.

GREEK TRAGEDY
It was classic, not a dry eye in the house.

EPISODE OF THREE STOOGES
I was Larry, trapped between Curly and Moe.

SOAP OPERA
I didn't think these things could happen, until it happened to me.

ACTION ADVENTURE
When I rode onto the scene, everybody noticed.

BIBLE EPIC
Cecil B. DeMille couldn't have done it any better.

LATE NIGHT NEWS
It might as well have been broadcast over the airwaves.

BORING LECTURE
The biggest challenge of the day was staying awake.

PROFESSIONAL WRESTLING MATCH
I feel as if Hulk Hogan's been coming after me.

FIREWORKS DISPLAY
It was spectacular.

# Music in My Life

Put an *"X"* on the first line below—somewhere between the two extremes—to indicate how you are feeling right now. Share your answers, and then repeat this process down the list. If you feel comfortable, briefly explain your response.

IN MY PERSONAL LIFE, I'M FEELING LIKE ...
**Blues in the Night** ______________________________ **Feeling Groovy**

IN MY FAMILY LIFE, I'M FEELING LIKE ...
**Stormy Weather** ______________________________ **The Sound of Music**

IN MY EMOTIONAL LIFE, I'M FEELING LIKE ...
**The Feeling Is Gone** ______________________________ **On Eagle's Wings**

IN MY WORK, SCHOOL OR CAREER, I'M FEELING LIKE ...
**Take This Job and Shove It** ______________________________ **The Future's So Bright I Gotta Wear Shades**

IN MY SPIRITUAL LIFE, I'M FEELING LIKE ...
**Sounds of Silence** ______________________________ **Hallelujah Chorus**

# My Childhood Table

Try to recall the table where you ate most of your meals as a child, and the people who sat around that table. Use the questions below to describe these significant relationships, and how they helped to shape the person you are today.

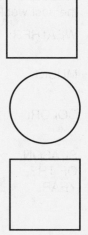

1. What was the shape of the table?
2. Where did you sit?
3. Who else was at the table?
4. If you had to describe each person with a color, what would be the color of (for instance):
   - ❐ Your father? (e.g., dark blue, because he was conservative like IBM)
   - ❐ Your mother? (e.g., light green, because she reminded me of springtime)
5. If you had to describe the atmosphere at the table with a color, what would you choose? (e.g., bright orange, because it was warm and light)
6. Who was the person at the table who praised you and made you feel special?
7. Who provided the spiritual leadership in your home?

## Home Improvement

Take inventory of your own life. Bob Munger, in his booklet *My Heart—Christ's Home*, describes the areas of a person's life as the rooms of a house. Give yourself a grade on each room as follows, then share with the others your best and worst grade.

- ❒ A = excellent
- ❒ B = good
- ❒ C = passing, needs a little dusting
- ❒ D = passing, but needs a lot of improvement

LIBRARY: This room is in your mind—what you allow to go into it and come out of it. It is the "control room" of the entire house.

DINING ROOM: Appetites, desires; those things your mind and spirit feed on for nourishment.

DRAWING ROOM: This is where you draw close to God—seeking time with him daily, not just in times of distress or need.

WORKSHOP: This room is where your gifts, talents and skills are put to work for God—by the power of the Spirit.

RUMPUS ROOM: The social area of your life; the things you do to amuse yourself and others.

HALL CLOSET: The one secret place that no one knows about, but is a real stumbling block in your walk in the Spirit.

## How Is It With Your Soul?

John Wesley, the founder of the Methodist Church, asked his "class meetings" to check in each week at their small group meeting with this question: "How is it with your soul?" To answer this question, choose one of these four allegories to explain the past week in your life:

WEATHER: For example: "This week has been mostly cloudy, with some thunderstorms at midweek. Right now, the weather is a little brighter ..."

MUSIC: For example: "This past week has been like heavy rock music—almost too loud. The sound seems to reverberate off the walls."

COLOR: For example: "This past week has been mostly fall colors—deep orange, flaming red and pumpkin."

SEASON OF THE YEAR: For example: "This past week has been like springtime. New signs of life are beginning to appear on the barren trees, and a few shoots of winter wheat are breaking through the frozen ground."

## My Spiritual Journey

The half-finished sentences below are designed to help you share your spiritual story. Ask one person to finish all the sentences. Then move to the next person, etc. If you are short on time, have only one person tell their story in this session.

1. RELIGIOUS BACKGROUND: My spiritual story begins in my home as a child, where the religious training was ...

2. CHURCH: The church that I went to as a child was ...

3. SIGNIFICANT PERSON: The person who had the greatest influence on my spiritual formation was ...

4. PERSONAL ENCOUNTER: The first time God became more than just a name to me was when ...

5. JOURNEY: Since my personal encounter with God, my Christian life might be described as ...

6. PRESENT: On a scale from 1 to 10, I would describe my spiritual energy level right now as a ...

7. NEXT STEP: The thing I need to work on right now in my spiritual life is ...

## Bragging Rights

Check your group for bragging rights in these categories.

- ❒ SPEEDING TICKETS: the person with the most speeding tickets
- ❒ BROKEN BONES: the person with the most broken bones
- ❒ STITCHES: the person with the most stitches
- ❒ SCARS: the person with the longest scar
- ❒ FISH OR GAME: the person who claims they caught the largest fish or killed the largest animal
- ❒ STUNTS: the person with the most death-defying story
- ❒ IRON: the person who can pump the most iron

# Personal Habits

Have everyone in your group finish the sentence on the first category by putting an "***X***" somewhere between the two extremes (e.g., on HOUSEWORK ... I would put myself closer to "Where's the floor?"). Repeat this process down the list as time permits.

ON HOUSEWORK, I AM SOMEWHERE BETWEEN:
**Eat off the floor**______________________________**Where's the floor?**

ON COOKING, I AM SOMEWHERE BETWEEN:
**Every meal is an act of worship**______________________________**Make it fast and hold the frills**

ON EXERCISING, I AM SOMEWHERE BETWEEN:
**Workout every morning**______________________________**Click the remote**

ON SHOPPING, I AM SOMEWHERE BETWEEN:
**Shop all day for a bargain**______________________________**Only the best**

ON EATING, I AM SOMEWHERE BETWEEN:
**You are what you eat**______________________________**Eat, drink and be merry**

# American Graffiti

If Hollywood made a movie about your life on the night of your high school prom, what would be needed? Let each person in your group have a few minutes to recall these details. If you have more than four or five in your group, ask everyone to choose two or three topics to talk about.

1. LOCATION: Where were you living?
2. WEIGHT: How much did you weigh—soaking wet?
3. PROM: Where was it held?
4. DATE: Who did you go with?
5. CAR / TRANSPORTATION: How did you get there? (If you used a car, what was the model, year, color, condition?)
6. ATTIRE: What did you wear?
7. PROGRAM: What was the entertainment?
8. AFTERWARD: What did you do afterward?
9. HIGHLIGHT: What was the highlight of the evening?
10. HOMECOMING: If you could go back and visit your high school, who would you like to see?

# Group Orchestra

Read out loud the first item and let everyone nominate the person in your group for this musical instrument in your group orchestra. Then, read aloud the next instrument, and call out another name, etc.

ANGELIC HARP: Soft, gentle, melodious, wooing with heavenly sounds.

OLD-FASHIONED WASHBOARD: Nonconforming, childlike and fun.

PLAYER PIANO: Mischievous, raucous, honky-tonk—delightfully carefree.

KETTLEDRUM: Strong, vibrant, commanding when needed but usually in the background.

PASSIONATE CASTANET: Full of Spanish fervor—intense and always upbeat.

STRADIVARIUS VIOLIN: Priceless, exquisite, soul-piercing—with the touch of the master.

FLUTTERING FLUTE: Tender, lighthearted, wide-ranging and clear as crystal.

SCOTTISH BAGPIPES: Forthright, distinctive and unmistakable.

SQUARE DANCE FIDDLE: Folksy, down-to-earth, toe-tapping—sprightly and full of energy.

ENCHANTING OBOE: Haunting, charming, disarming—even the cobra is harmless with this sound.

MELLOW CELLO: Deep, sonorous, compassionate—adding body and depth to the orchestra.

PIPE ORGAN: Grand, magnificent, rich—versatile and commanding.

HERALDING TRUMPET: Stirring, lively, invigorating—signaling attention and attack.

CLASSICAL GUITAR: Contemplative, profound, thoughtful *and* thought-provoking.

ONE-MAN BAND: Able to do many things well, all at once.

COMB AND TISSUE PAPER: Makeshift, original, uncomplicated—homespun and creative.

SWINGING TROMBONE: Warm, rich—great in solo or background support.

# Broadway Show

Imagine for a moment that your group has been chosen to produce a Broadway show, and you have to choose people from your group for all of the jobs for this production. Have someone read out loud the job description for the first job below—PRODUCER. Then, let everyone in your group call out the name of the person in your group who would best fit this job. (You don't have to agree.) Then read the job description for the next job and let everyone nominate another person, etc. You only have 10 minutes for this assignment, so move fast.

PRODUCER: Typical Hollywood business tycoon; extravagant, big-budget, big-production magnate in the Steven Spielberg style.

DIRECTOR: Creative, imaginative brains who coordinates the production and draws the best out of others.

HEROINE: Beautiful, captivating, everybody's heart throb; defenseless when men are around, but nobody's fool.

HERO: Tough, macho, champion of the underdog, knight in shining armor; defender of truth.

COMEDIAN: Childlike, happy-go-lucky, outrageously funny, keeps everyone laughing.

CHARACTER PERSON: Rugged individualist, outrageously different, colorful, adds spice to any surrounding.

FALL GUY: Easy-going, nonchalant character who wins the hearts of everyone by being the "foil" of the heavy characters.

TECHNICAL DIRECTOR: The genius for "sound and lights"; creates the perfect atmosphere.

COMPOSER OF LYRICS: Communicates in music what everybody understands; heavy into feelings, moods, outbursts of energy.

PUBLICITY AGENT: Advertising and public relations expert; knows all the angles, good at one-liners, a flair for "hot" news.

VILLAIN: The "bad guy" who really is the heavy for the plot, forces others to think, challenges traditional values; out to destroy anything artificial or hypocritical.

AUTHOR: Shy, aloof; very much in touch with feelings, sensitive to people, puts into words what others only feel.

STAGEHAND: Supportive, behind-the-scenes person who makes things run smoothly; patient and tolerant.

# Wild Predictions

Try to match the people in your group to the crazy forecasts below. (Don't take it too seriously; it's meant to be fun!) Read out loud the first item and ask everyone to call out the name of the person who is most likely to accomplish this feat. Then, read the next item and ask everyone to make a new prediction, etc.

THE PERSON IN OUR GROUP MOST LIKELY TO ...

Make a million selling Beanie Babies over the Internet

Become famous for designing new attire for sumo wrestlers

Replace Vanna White on *Wheel of Fortune*

Appear on *The Tonight Show* to exhibit an acrobatic talent

Move to a desert island

Discover a new use for underarm deodorant

Succeed David Letterman as host of *The Late Show*

Substitute for John Madden as Fox's football color analyst

Appear on the cover of *Muscle & Fitness Magazine*

Become the newest member of the Spice Girls

Work as a bodyguard for Rush Limbaugh at Feminist convention

Write a best-selling novel based on their love life

Be a dance instructor on a cruise ship for wealthy, well-endowed widows

Win the blue ribbon at the state fair for best Rocky Mountain oyster recipe

Land a job as head librarian for Amazon.com

Be the first woman to win the Indianapolis 500

Open the Clouseau Private Detective Agency

# Career Placements

Read the list of career choices aloud and quickly choose someone in your group for each job—based upon their unique gifts and talents. Have fun!

SPACE ENVIRONMENTAL ENGINEER: in charge of designing the bathrooms on space shuttles

SCHOOL BUS DRIVER: for junior high kids in New York City (earplugs supplied)

WRITER: of an "advice to the lovelorn" column in Hollywood

SUPERVISOR: of a complaint department for a large automobile dealership and service department

ANIMAL PSYCHIATRIST: for French poodles in a fashionable suburb of Paris

RESEARCH SCIENTIST: studying the fertilization patterns of the dodo bird—now extinct

SAFARI GUIDE: in the heart of Africa—for wealthy widows and eccentric bachelors

LITTLE LEAGUE BASEBALL COACH: in Mudville, Illinois—last year's record was 0 and 12

MANAGER: of your local McDonald's during the holiday rush with 210 teenage employees

LIBRARIAN: for the Walt Disney Hall of Fame memorabilia

CHOREOGRAPHER: for the Dallas Cowboys cheerleaders

NURSE'S AIDE: at a home for retired Sumo wrestlers

SECURITY GUARD: crowd control officer at a rock concert

ORGANIZER: of paperwork for Congress

PUBLIC RELATIONS MANAGER: for Dennis Rodman

BODYGUARD: for Rush Limbaugh on a speaking tour of feminist groups

TOY ASSEMBLY PERSON: for a toy store over the holidays

# You and Me, Partner

Think of the people in your group as you read over the list of activities below. If you had to choose someone from your group to be your partner, who would you choose to do these activities with? Jot down each person's name beside the activity. You can use each person's name only once and you have to use everyone's name once—so think it through before you jot down their names. Then, let one person listen to what others chose for them. Then, move to the next person, etc., around your group.

WHO WOULD YOU CHOOSE FOR THE FOLLOWING?

_______________ ENDURANCE DANCE CONTEST partner

_______________ BOBSLED RACE partner for the Olympics

_______________ TRAPEZE ACT partner

_______________ MY UNDERSTUDY for my debut in a Broadway musical

_______________ BEST MAN or MAID OF HONOR at my wedding

_______________ SECRET UNDERCOVER AGENT copartner

_______________ BODYGUARD for me when I strike it rich

_______________ MOUNTAIN CLIMBING partner in climbing Mt. Everest

_______________ ASTRONAUT to fly the space shuttle while I walk in space

_______________ SAND CASTLE TOURNAMENT building partner

_______________ PIT CREW foreman for entry in Indianapolis 500

_______________ AUTHOR for my biography

_______________ SURGEON to operate on me for a life-threatening cancer

_______________ NEW BUSINESS START-UP partner

_______________ TAG-TEAM partner for a professional wrestling match

_______________ HEAVY-DUTY PRAYER partner

# My Gourmet Group

Here's a chance to pass out some much deserved praise for the people who have made your group something special. Ask one person to sit in silence while the others explain the delicacy they would choose to describe the contribution this person has made to your group. Repeat the process for each member of the group.

CAVIAR: That special touch of class and aristocratic taste that has made the rest of us feel like royalty.

PRIME RIB: Stable, brawny, macho, the generous mainstay of any menu; juicy, mouth-watering "perfect cut" for good nourishment.

IMPORTED CHEESE: Distinctive, tangy, mellow with age; adds depth to any meal.

VINEGAR AND OIL: Tart, witty, dry; a rare combination of healing ointment and pungent spice to add "bite" to the salad.

ARTICHOKE HEARTS: Tender and disarmingly vulnerable; whets the appetite for heartfelt sharing.

FRENCH PASTRY: Tempting, irresistible "creme de la creme" dessert; the connoisseur's delight for topping off a meal.

PHEASANT UNDER GLASS: Wild, totally unique, a rare dish for people who appreciate original fare.

CARAFE OF WINE: Sparkling, effervescent, exuberant and joyful; outrageously free and liberating to the rest of us.

ESCARGOT AND OYSTERS: Priceless treasures of the sea once out of their shells; succulent, delicate and irreplaceable.

FRESH FRUIT: Vine-ripened, energy-filled, invigorating; the perfect treat after a heavy meal.

ITALIAN ICE CREAMS: Colorful, flavorful, delightfully childlike; the unexpected surprise in our group.

# Thank You

How would you describe your experience with this group? Choose one of the animals below that best describes how your experience in this group affected your life. Then share your responses with the group.

WILD EAGLE: You have helped to heal my wings, and taught me how to soar again.

TOWERING GIRAFFE: You have helped me to hold my head up and stick my neck out, and reach over the fences I have built.

PLAYFUL PORPOISE: You have helped me to find a new freedom and a whole new world to play in.

COLORFUL PEACOCK: You have told me that I'm beautiful; I've started to believe it, and it's changing my life.

SAFARI ELEPHANT: I have enjoyed this new adventure, and I'm not going to forget it, or this group; I can hardly wait for the next safari.

LOVABLE HIPPOPOTAMUS: You have let me surface and bask in the warm sunshine of God's love.

LANKY LEOPARD: You have helped me to look closely at myself and see some spots, and you still accept me the way I am.

DANCING BEAR: You have taught me to dance in the midst of pain, and you have helped me to reach out and hug again.

ALL-WEATHER DUCK: You have helped me to celebrate life—even in stormy weather—and to sing in the rain.

# Academy Awards

You have had a chance to observe the gifts and talents of the members of your group. Now you will have a chance to pass out some much deserved praise for the contribution that each member of the group has made to your life. Read out loud the first award. Then let everyone nominate the person they feel is the most deserving for that award. Then read the next award, etc., through the list. Have fun!

SPARK PLUG AWARD: for the person who ignited the group

DEAR ABBY AWARD: for the person who cared enough to listen

ROYAL GIRDLE AWARD: for the person who supported us

WINNIE THE POOH AWARD: for the warm, caring person when someone needed a hug

ROCK OF GIBRALTER AWARD: for the person who was strong in the tough times of our group

OPRAH AWARD: for the person who asked the fun questions that got us to talk

TED KOPPEL AWARD: for the person who asked the heavy questions that made us think

KING ARTHUR'S AWARD: for the knight in shining armor

PINK PANTHER AWARD: for the detective who made us deal with Scripture

NOBEL PEACE PRIZE: for the person who harmonized our differences of opinion without diminishing anyone

BIG MAC AWARD: for the person who showed the biggest hunger for spiritual things

SERENDIPITY CROWN: for the person who grew the most spiritually during the course—in your estimation

# You Remind Me of Jesus

Every Christian reflects the character of Jesus in some way. As your group has gotten to know each other, you can begin to see how each person demonstrates Christ in their very own personality. Go around the circle and have each person listen while others take turns telling that person what they notice in him or her that reminds them of Jesus. You may also want to tell them why you selected what you did.

YOU REMIND ME OF ...

JESUS THE HEALER: You seem to be able to touch someone's life with your compassion and help make them whole.

JESUS THE SERVANT: There's nothing that you wouldn't do for someone.

JESUS THE PREACHER: You share your faith in a way that challenges and inspires people.

JESUS THE LEADER: As Jesus had a plan for the disciples, you are able to lead others in a way that honors God.

JESUS THE REBEL: By doing the unexpected, you remind me of Jesus' way of revealing God in unique, surprising ways.

JESUS THE RECONCILER: Like Jesus, you have the ability to be a peacemaker between others.

JESUS THE TEACHER: You have a gift for bringing light and understanding to God's Word.

JESUS THE CRITIC: You have the courage to say what needs to be said, even if it isn't always popular.

JESUS THE SACRIFICE: Like Jesus, you seem willing to sacrifice anything to glorify God.

# Reflections

Take some time to evaluate the life of your group by using the statements below. Read the first sentence out loud and ask everyone to explain where they would put a dot between the two extremes. When you are finished, go back and give your group an overall grade in the category of Group Building, Bible Study and Mission.

## GROUP BUILDING

On celebrating life and having fun together, we were more like a ...

**wet blanket** ________________________________________ **hot tub**

On becoming a caring community, we were more like a ...

**prickly porcupine** ________________________________________ **cuddly teddy bear**

## SPIRITUAL FORMATION (Bible Study)

On sharing our spiritual stories, we were more like a ...

**shallow pond** ________________________________________ **spring-fed lake**

On digging into Scripture, we were more like a ...

**slow-moving snail** ________________________________________ **voracious anteater**

## MISSION

On inviting new people into our group, we were more like a ...

**barbed-wire fence** ________________________________________ **wide-open door**

On stretching our vision for mission, we were more like an ...

**ostrich** ________________________________________ **eagle**

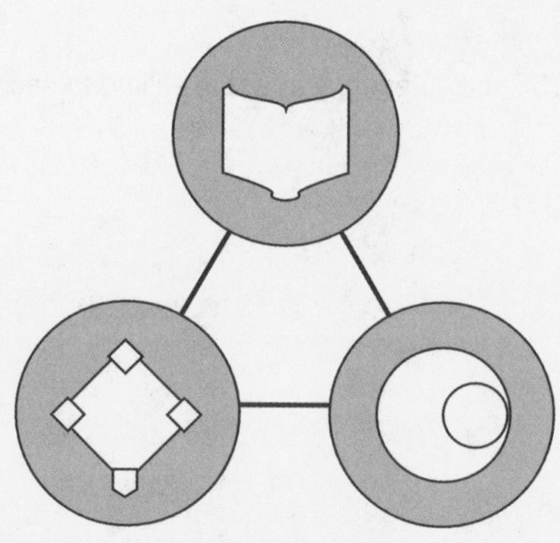

# Human Bingo / Party Mixer

After the leader says "Go!" circulate the room, asking people the things described in the boxes. If someone answers "Yes" to a question, have them sign their initials in that box. Continue until someone completes the entire card—or one row if you don't have that much time. You can only use someone's name twice, and you cannot use your own name on your card.

| | | | | | | |
|---|---|---|---|---|---|---|
| can juggle | TP'd a house | never used an outhouse | sings in the shower | rec'd 6+ traffic tickets | paddled in school | watches Sesame Street |
| sleeps in church regularly | never changed a diaper | split pants in public | milked a cow | born out of the country | has been to Hawaii | can do the splits |
| watches soap operas | can touch tongue to nose | rode a motor-cycle | never ridden a horse | moved twice last year | sleeps on a waterbed | has hole in sock |
| walked in wrong restroom | loves classical music | skipped school | **FREE** | broke a leg | has a hot tub | loves eating sushi |
| is an only child | loves raw oysters | has a 3-inch + scar | doesn't wear PJ's | smoked a cigar | can dance the Charleston | weighs under 110 lbs. |
| likes writing poetry | still has tonsils | loves crossword puzzles | likes bubble baths | wearing Fruit of the Loom | doesn't use mouth-wash | often watches cartoons |
| kissed on first date | can wiggle ears | can play the guitar | plays chess regularly | reads the comics first | can touch palms to floor | sleeps with stuffed animal |

# Group Covenant

Any group can benefit from creating a group covenant. Reserve some time during one of the first meetings to discuss answers to the following questions. When everyone in the group has the same expectations for the group, everything runs more smoothly.

1. The purpose of our group is:

2. The goals of our group are:

3. We will meet for ______ weeks, after which we will decide if we wish to continue as a group. If we do decide to continue, we will reconsider this covenant.

4. We will meet __________________ (weekly, every other week, monthly).

5. Our meetings will be from _________ o'clock to _________ o'clock, and we will strive to start and end on time.

6. We will meet at __________________________________________________ or rotate from house to house.

7. We will take care of the following details: ❒ child care ❒ refreshments

8. We agree to the following rules for our group:

   ❒ PRIORITY: While we are in this group, group meetings have priority.

   ❒ PARTICIPATION: Everyone is given the right to their own opinion and all questions are respected.

   ❒ CONFIDENTIALITY: Anything said in the meeting is not to be repeated outside the meeting.

   ❒ EMPTY CHAIR: The group stays open to new people and invites prospective members to visit the group.

   ❒ SUPPORT: Permission is given to call each other in times of need.

   ❒ ADVICE GIVING: Unsolicited advice is not allowed.

   ❒ MISSION: We will do all that is in our power to start a new group.

of control. It only took a "small spark" to create a huge conflagration.

**3:6** This is a notoriously difficult verse to translate and to understand. The general sense, however, is clear. The tongue is like a fire. It is capable of corrupting the whole person. Speech can burst forth into evil action.

***a world of evil.*** As in 1:27, the "world" is that which stands in opposition to God. The tongue is, potentially, a force for evil. "The idea is, presumably, that it is in his speech that a man identifies himself with that total hostility to God, and shows that it is part of his inner character (cf. Mark 7:20)" (Laws).

***hell.*** Literally *Gehenna*, a ravine south of Jerusalem where the garbage was burned. It became a metaphor for the place of punishment. These evil words find their inspiration and source in hell itself.

**3:7** ***reptiles.*** In the Greco-Roman world, serpents were thought to have healing power, and so the ill slept among tame snakes in the temples of Aesculapius. The modern symbol used by the medical profession has a snake entwined around a shaft.

**3:8** ***tame.*** The Old Testament states that one of the functions of human beings is to domesticate the animal kingdom (see Gen. 1:28; 9:2; Ps. 8:6–8). Yet despite our ability to control all four classes of animals (mammals, birds, amphibians and fish), we remain unable to subdue our own tongues.

***restless.*** The same word is also used in 1:8 and is translated there as "unstable." It is used to describe the double-minded person. In 3:9, the dual nature of the tongue will be emphasized.

***deadly poison.*** As with serpents, so human tongues can bring death as well (see Ps. 58:3–5; 140:3).

***Despite our ability to control all four classes of animals (mammals, birds, amphibians and fish), we remain unable to subdue our own tongues.***

**3:9** ***With the tongue we praise.*** The tongue is vital to all worship: praying, singing, praising and thanking. Devout Jews offered praise to God three times a day.

***we curse men.*** Everybody, even James, has the same problem with the tongue. It is by means of words that people bring real harm to others.

***in God's likeness.*** Since people are made in the image of God, when they are cursed, God too is being cursed. The same tongue that praises God is also used to curse him, a point James makes explicit in verse 10.

**3:11–12** James ends with three illustrations from nature which show how unnatural it is for human beings to use the same vehicle to utter praises and curses. Nothing in nature is like that, he says. A spring gives one type of water only—fresh water or brackish water. A tree bears only a single species of fruit.

# 7 Kinds of Wisdom—James 3:13–18

## THREE-PART AGENDA

**ICE-BREAKER**
15 Minutes

**BIBLE STUDY**
30 Minutes

**CARING TIME**
15–45 Minutes

***LEADER: Have you started working with your group about your mission—for instance, by having them review pages M3 and M6 in the center section? If you have a new person at the meeting, remember to do an appropriate ice-breaker from the center section.***

## TO BEGIN THE BIBLE STUDY TIME

(Choose 1 or 2)

1. Growing up, how did your parents resolve disputes between you and your sibling(s)?
2. What subject or topic do you like to research and gather information on?
3. Who is someone you admire as a "peacemaker"?

## READ SCRIPTURE & DISCUSS

(If you don't have time for all the questions in this section, conclude the Bible Study [30 min.] by answering question #7.)

1. When someone gives you advice, how do you determine whether it is good or bad?
2. How is "wisdom" generally defined in our society?
3. What are the characteristics of "earthly" wisdom? What happens when earthly wisdom is pursued?
4. When have envy and selfish ambition affected your life?

Two Kinds of Wisdom

[13]***Who is wise and understanding among you? Let him show it by his good life, by deeds done in the humility that comes from wisdom.*** [14]***But if you harbor bitter envy and selfish ambition in your hearts, do not boast about it or deny the truth.*** [15]***Such "wisdom" does not come down from heaven but is earthly, unspiritual, of the devil.*** [16]***For where you have envy and selfish ambition, there you find disorder and every evil practice.***

[17]***But the wisdom that comes from heaven is first of all pure; then peace-loving, considerate, submissive, full of mercy and good fruit, impartial and sincere.*** [18]***Peacemakers who sow in peace raise a harvest of righteousness.***

5. What characteristics show that a person possesses true, "heavenly" wisdom? Where do you most need this kind of wisdom?
6. What qualities in verse 17 do you most need to develop in your life?
7. In what situation do you need to sow seeds of peace?

## CARING TIME

(Choose 1 or 2 of these questions before closing in prayer. Be sure to pray for the empty chair.)

1. What is your dream for the future mission of this group?
2. Rate the past week on a scale of 1 (terrible) to 10 (great). What's the outlook for this week?
3. How can the group pray for you in the coming week?

# Notes—James 3:13–18

**Summary.** This is part two of James' discussion of wisdom. In it, he probes why on the one hand speech can be so destructive—yet on the other hand, there are teachers in the church (of whom he is one) who communicate true wisdom. His conclusion is that it all depends on the *source* of the words. In this session, he distinguishes between wisdom from above and wisdom from below. This session not only looks backward to the problem of destructive speech (3:1–12), but it also looks forward to the problem such uncontrolled speech has brought to the Christian community—the issue James will deal with in the next section (4:1–12).

***True wisdom will show itself via a good life filled with loving deeds done in a humble spirit. But envy and ambition will display itself by quite a different sort of life.***

***True wisdom produces right relationships between people.***

**3:13 *Who is wise ... among you?*** James is probably thinking of the problem of false teachers which he raised in 3:1. Yet given the fact that wisdom is a major theme of this book as he indicated in his introduction (see 1:5–8,16–21), these words are also intended for all Christians to hear and heed.

***Let him show it.*** The same problem faces the Christian who claims to have "faith," as faces the one who claims to have "understanding." Both of these qualities are interior. Neither can be seen directly. Both must be demonstrated. As James argued in chapter two, faith is shown via the deeds it inspires. But how is understanding shown?

***by his good life, by deeds.*** It might be anticipated that understanding would be demonstrated by means of speech. Those who had the most understanding would possess the best verbal skills. They would be the popular teachers or the clever debaters. But this is not what James says. Understanding, like faith, is shown by *how one lives.* Specifically, understanding is demonstrated by a good life and by good deeds. Those who truly "understand" will live the kind of life that displays such understanding. This is also what Jesus taught (see Matt. 7:15–23.)

***humility.*** Contemporary Greek culture considered this to be a negative characteristic, fit only for slaves and characterized by abject groveling. It was Christians who came to understand how crucial humility was for harmonious relationships. A humble person will not need to make a point of how wise they are, and will not have to defend themselves. Conflict is defused because the humble person has no need to establish a reputation over against other people. As James will show in 3:17–18, humility is also necessary for peace which is itself a characteristic of true wisdom.

***wisdom.*** These deeds arise not only from humility but also from wisdom and so they display for all to see the fact of this inner understanding or wisdom.

**3:14–16** Having described how true wisdom shows itself, James now turns to a description of how "pretend" wisdom displays itself. James is concerned to show his readers that any claim to wisdom is vitiated by such behavior as he describes: it becomes a "non-wisdom." His point is not that there is a different wisdom in opposition to the true one, but that a claim to true wisdom cannot be upheld in the context of an inconsistent style of life (Laws).

**3:14** Envy and ambition are the marks of false teachers. James is probably referring to the teachers he mentioned in 3:1 who are rivals vying for positions of authority within the Jerusalem church. Such competition clearly violates the nature of wisdom.

***bitter envy.*** The word translated "bitter" is the same word which was used in verse 12 to describe brackish water unfit for human consumption. It is now applied to zeal (the word translated "envy" is literally *zelos*). Zeal that has gone astray becomes jealousy.

***selfish ambition.*** The word translated here as "selfish ambition" originally meant "those who can be hired to do spinning." Then it came to mean "those who work for pay." It later came to mean "those who work only for what they get out of it" and it was applied to those who sought political office merely for personal gain (Barclay).

***in your hearts.*** This is the issue: What lies at the core of the person's being? Is it true wisdom from God or is it ambition? True wisdom will show itself via a good life filled with loving deeds done in a humble spirit. But envy and ambition will display itself by quite a different sort of life (which James will describe more fully in v. 16).

***do not boast about it or deny the truth.*** Those whose hearts are filled with this sense of rivalry and party spirit ought not to pretend that they are speaking God's wisdom. That is merely to compound the wrong.

**3:15** James uses three terms—each of which is less desirable than the previous one—to describe the true origin of this "non-wisdom." There is "earthly" wisdom which arises out of this world. There is "unspiritual" wisdom which arises out of the "soul" of the person. Neither form of wisdom is necessarily bad, except when it claims to originate with the Spirit of God. And then there is wisdom "of the devil" which is not neutral. This is literally, "demon-like"; i.e., that which is possessed even by demons (see 2:19) or which is under the control of evil spirits.

**3:16–18** James contrasts the lifestyle that emerges from pretend wisdom (v. 16) with that which arises out of true wisdom (vv. 17–18).

**3:17 *wisdom.*** "Nothing is said about an intellectual or doctrinal content for wisdom. ... Wisdom is understood in terms of moral virtue and practical goodness" (Laws).

***pure.*** The Greek word describes a sort of moral purity that enables one to approach the "gods." This is "wisdom which is so cleansed of all ulterior motives, so cleansed of self, that it has become pure enough to see God" (Barclay).

***peace-loving.*** This is the opposite of envy and ambition. True wisdom produces right relationships between people, which is the root idea behind the word "peace" when it is used in the New Testament.

***considerate.*** This is a very difficult word to translate into English. It has the sense of that "which steps in to correct things when the law itself has become unjust" as Aristotle put it. True wisdom will cause a person to be equitable and to make allowances, rather than always insisting in a harsh way on the letter of the law. At other places in the New Testament this word is translated as "gentle" (see Phil. 4:5 and 1 Tim. 3:3).

***submissive.*** Though this Greek word can be translated (as the NIV has done) to have the sense of "a willingness to obey God," it probably should be understood in its second sense of "willingness to be persuaded," since it follows the word "considerate." True wisdom is willing to listen, learn and then yield when persuaded.

***full of mercy and good fruit.*** Christian mercy (compassion) is extended even to those whose troubles are their own fault and is demonstrated by concrete action ("good fruit") and not just by an emotional response. True wisdom reaches out to the unfortunate in practical ways, a point James never tires of making.

***impartial.*** Literally, "undivided"; that is, true wisdom does not vacillate back and forth. It is the opposite of the wavering person in 1:6–8.

***sincere.*** True wisdom does not act or pretend. It is honest and genuine.

***True wisdom reaches out to the unfortunate in practical ways.***

***True wisdom will cause a person to be equitable and to make allowances, rather than always insisting in a harsh way on the letter of the law.***

**3:18** "James' argument ... runs as follows: There is not wisdom where there is divisiveness, for wisdom is peaceable; it is the peacemakers, then, who possess wisdom, which is the fruit of righteousness" (Laws). Peace flows from true wisdom in contrast to the sort of harsh insistence on "truth" that divides people.

# 8 Submit to God—James 4:1–12

## THREE-PART AGENDA

| ICE-BREAKER | BIBLE STUDY | CARING TIME |
|---|---|---|
| 15 Minutes | 30 Minutes | 15–45 Minutes |

***LEADER: To help you identify an Apprentice / Leader for a new small group (or if you have a new person at this meeting), see the listing of ice-breakers on page M7 of the center section.***

## TO BEGIN THE BIBLE STUDY TIME

(Choose 1 or 2)

1. If you were a judge at the Olympics, what event would you want to be involved with?
2. Growing up, who did you quarrel with the most? Over what?
3. If you were granted "one wish," what would you wish for?

## READ SCRIPTURE & DISCUSS

(If you don't have time for all the questions in this section, conclude the Bible Study [30 min.] by answering question #7.)

1. When comparing yourself to others, what do you envy most: Hair? Clothes? Car? House? Other?
2. What is at the root of fights and quarrels?
3. What are two reasons we don't have what we want? What might some other reasons be for unanswered prayer?
4. What is "friendship with the world" (v. 4)? How are you most likely to fall into loyalty to this "friend"?
5. What "desires" seem to drive the world around us? What can we do to overcome the lure of the world?

Submit Yourselves to God

**4** ***What causes fights and quarrels among you? Don't they come from your desires that battle within you?***
***2 You want something but don't get it. You kill and covet, but you cannot have what you want. You quarrel and fight. You do not have, because you do not ask God. 3 When you ask, you do not receive, because you ask with wrong motives, that you may spend what you get on your pleasures.***

***4 You adulterous people, don't you know that friendship with the world is hatred toward God? Anyone who chooses to be a friend of the world becomes an enemy of God. 5 Or do you think Scripture says without reason that the spirit he caused to live in us envies intensely?***[a] ***6 But he gives us more grace. That is why Scripture says:***

> ***"God opposes the proud***
> ***but gives grace to the humble."***[b]

***7 Submit yourselves, then, to God. Resist the devil, and he will flee from you. 8 Come near to God and he will come near to you. Wash your hands, you sinners, and purify your hearts, you double-minded. 9 Grieve, mourn and wail. Change your laughter to mourning and your joy to gloom.***
***10 Humble yourselves before the Lord, and he will lift you up.***

***11 Brothers, do not slander one another. Anyone who speaks against his brother or judges him speaks against the law and judges it. When you judge the law, you are not keeping it, but sitting in judgment on it. 12 There is only one Lawgiver and Judge, the one who is able to save and destroy. But you—who are you to judge your neighbor?***

[a] 5 Or *that God jealously longs for the spirit that he made to live in us;* or *that the Spirit he caused to live in us longs jealously*  [b] 6 Prov. 3:34

6. How does following verses 7–10 improve our relationship with God?
7. Where do you need to experience God's grace in your life this week?

## CARING TIME

(Choose 1 or 2 of these questions before closing in prayer. Be sure to pray for the empty chair.)

1. How was the weather in your spiritual life last week: Sunny and warm? Scattered showers? Cold and snowy? Other? What's the forecast for the coming week?
2. Have you started working on your group mission—to choose an Apprentice / Leader from this group to start a new group in the future? (See Mission / Multiplication on p. M3.)
3. In what specific way can the group pray for you this week?

# Notes—James 4:1–12

**Summary.** The third and final part of James' discussion about wisdom has to do with their life together as a church. Their failure to live out God's wisdom has had the most serious consequences for them as a community of believers.

**4:1–3** James begins by naming the root cause of all this strife. It is the desire for pleasure.

**4:1 *What causes fights and quarrels among you?*** Where does all this strife come from? It is not initiated by the wise leaders who are peacemakers (3:18). It is not caused by persecution from the world. James is very clear that the strife is internal ("among you").

***fights and quarrels.*** Literally, "wars and battles." These are long-term conflicts, not sudden explosions.

***desires.*** Literally, "pleasures." In Greek the word is *hedone,* from which our word "hedonism" is derived. James is not saying that personal pleasure is inherently wrong. However, there is a certain desire for gratification that springs from the wrong source and possesses a person in the pursuit of its fulfillment.

***battle.*** The human personality is pictured as having been invaded by an alien army. "Human nature is indeed in the grip of an overwhelming army of occupation. Its natural aim, it can be truthfully said, is pleasure; and when we consider the amount of time, energy, money, interest and enthusiasm that men and women give to the satisfaction of this aim we can appreciate the accuracy of James' diagnosis; and Christians can use it as reliable yardstick by which to measure the sincerity of their religion. Is God or pleasure the dominant concern of their life" (Tasker)?

***within you.*** The struggle is within a person—between the part of him or her which is controlled by the Holy Spirit and that which is controlled by the world.

**4:2 *You want something.*** This is desire at work (see 1:14).

***but don't get it.*** This is desire frustrated.

***kill and covet.*** This is how frustrated desire responds. It lashes out at others in anger and abuse. (This is "killing" in a metaphorical sense—see Matt. 5:21–22.) It responds in jealousy to those who have what it wants.

***quarrel and fight.*** But still they do not have what they desire so the hostile action continues. This mad desire-driven quest causes a person to disregard other people, trampling over them if necessary to get what they want.

***you do not ask God.*** One reason for this frustrated desire is a lack of prayer.

***The struggle is within a person—between the part of him or her which is controlled by the Holy Spirit and that which is controlled by the world.***

**4:3** James senses a protest: "But I did ask God and I didn't get it." So he qualifies the absolute assertion in verse 2. The desire expressed in prayer may be inappropriate. God will not grant this type of request. Christians pray "in the name of Jesus," implying submission to the will of God. They can ask for wisdom and always expect to get it (if they do not waver), as James explains in 1:5. But this is different than asking for something to sate an illicit pleasure and expecting to get it. Prayer is not magic. The implication is not that God will not give us things that give us pleasure. God is the gracious God who gives not only bread and water but also steak and wine (see Phil. 4:12). The point is that they are motivated by selfish desires and ask simply to gratify themselves. This is not the trusting child asking for a meal but the greedy child asking for the best piece or the spoiled child demanding his or her way. They are asking God to bless their schemes; God will have no part of it (Davids, GNC).

***spend.*** This is the same word used in Luke 15:14 to describe the profligate behavior of the Prodigal Son.

**4:4 *adulterous people.*** In Greek, this word is feminine, *adulteresses*, and probably refers to the people of Israel. By extension it refers to the church, the new Israel. In the Old Testament it was common to picture the relationship between God and his people as similar to the relationship between a husband and his wife (Isa. 54:5). To give spiritual allegiance to another ("the world") is therefore expressed in terms of adultery.

**4:6** But their case is not hopeless. God does give grace. Repentance is possible. They can turn from their misbehavior.

***proud.*** Haughty and arrogant, to set oneself above others.

***grace.*** To receive grace, a person must *ask* for it. To be able to ask, one must see the need to do so. The proud person can't and doesn't see such a need. Only the humble do.

**4:7–10** By means of a series of 10 imperatives, James tells them how to repent. "Do this," he says, "and you will escape the mess you have gotten yourselves in." Thus, he tells them to submit, resist, come near, wash, purify, grieve, mourn, wail, change, and humble themselves.

***To receive grace, a person must ask for it. To be able to ask, one must see the need to do so. The proud person can't and doesn't see such a need. Only the humble do.***

**4:7 *Submit yourselves, then, to God.*** His first and primary command is that they must submit to God. It is not too surprising that James says this, since what these Christians have been doing is resisting God and his ways. As James just pointed out, it is the humble who receive God's grace. A proud person is unwilling to submit and therefore not open to grace, feeling that he or she needs nothing.

***Resist the devil.*** Submission to God begins with resistance to Satan. Thus far they have been giving in to the devil's enticements. A clear sign of their new lifestyle will be this inner resistance to devilish desires.

***he will flee from you.*** Since Satan has no ultimate power over a Christian, when resisted he can do little but withdraw.

**4:8 *Wash your hands.*** Originally this was a ritual requirement whereby one became ceremoniously clean in preparation for the worship of God (see Ex. 30:19–21). Now it is a symbol of the sort of inner purity God desires.

***sinners.*** Those whose lives have become more characteristic of the enemy than of God—lapsed or "worldly" Christians.

***double-minded.*** This is the parallel word to "sinners" and expresses nicely what life with two competing masters is like. God asks for singleness of purpose in His disciples.

**4:9 *mourn and wail.*** When people realize that they have been leading self-centered lives, in disobedience to God and harmful to others, they often feel overwhelming grief.

**4:10 *Humble.*** This last command urges humility before God as did the first command ("Submit to God").

**4:11–12** James ends his section on wisdom and speech by moving from a general call to repentance (vv. 7–10) to a specific form of wrongdoing that they must deal with—the sin of judgment and the pride that underlies it.

**4:11 *slander.*** This is to speak evil about other people in their absence so that they are unable to defend themselves. The word means both *false* accusation and harsh (though perhaps accurate) *criticism.*

***speaks against the law.*** When a person judges someone else, it is a violation of the royal law of love (2:8) and thus a criticism of that law because of the implicit assumption that the law is not fully true since it does not apply in this case.

**4:12 *one Lawgiver and Judge.*** To judge others is to take to oneself a prerogative belonging to God. God is the Judge (see Ps. 75:6–7) and the Lawgiver.

***neighbor.*** The Christian's duty to his or her neighbor is quite clear. It is to love, not judge.

# 9 Boasting—James 4:13–17

## THREE-PART AGENDA

**ICE-BREAKER**
15 Minutes

**BIBLE STUDY**
30 Minutes

**CARING TIME**
15–45 Minutes

***LEADER: To help you identify an Apprentice / Leader for a new small group (or if you have a new person at this meeting), see the listing of ice-breakers on page M7 of the center section.***

## TO BEGIN THE BIBLE STUDY TIME

(Choose 1 or 2)

1. What are your plans for the weekend?
2. Where would you like to live during your retirement years?
3. If you were to "brag" about something, what would it be?

## READ SCRIPTURE & DISCUSS

(If you don't have time for all the questions in this section, conclude the Bible Study [30 min.] by answering question #7.)

1. What plans have you made, only to have them fall apart at the last minute (e.g., travel, job change, moving, etc.)? How did you feel?
2. In what way are these verses contrary to the ways of the world?
3. How far into the future have you planned your life? What attitude should we have toward our plans?
4. What is wrong with a little boasting and bragging?
5. Do you tend to struggle more with the things you do, or the things you fail to do?

Boasting About Tomorrow

***[13]Now listen, you who say, "Today or tomorrow we will go to this or that city, spend a year there, carry on business and make money." [14]Why, you do not even know what will happen tomorrow. What is your life? You are a mist that appears for a little while and then vanishes. [15]Instead, you ought to say, "If it is the Lord's will, we will live and do this or that." [16]As it is, you boast and brag. All such boasting is evil. [17]Anyone, then, who knows the good he ought to do and doesn't do it, sins.***

6. On a scale of 1 (hardly ever) to 10 (always), how often do you pray about your plans and decisions before making them?
7. What does this passage say to you about the plans you are making for the future? Where do you need God's guidance?

## CARING TIME

(Choose 1 or 2 of these questions before closing in prayer. Be sure to pray for the empty chair.)

1. How is the group doing "fielding their positions" (as shown on the team roster, p. M5)?
2. If this group is helping to hold you accountable for something, how are you doing in that area? If not, what is something for which you would like this group to hold you accountable?
3. What prayer needs or praises would you like to share?

# Notes—James 4:13–17

**Summary.** James begins discussion of his third and final theme: testing. He will deal with this theme, at first, as it touches the issue of wealth. The problem is the difficulty that comes with being wealthy and the tensions this brings, both on a personal level and for the whole community. In this first part of his discussion (4:13–17), he looks at the situation of a group of Christian businessmen—in particular, at their "sins of omission."

**4:13** Boasting about what will happen tomorrow is another example of human arrogance. It is in the same category as judging one another (vv. 11–12). Judgment is arrogant because God is the only legitimate judge. Boasting about the future is arrogant because God is the only one who knows what will happen in the future.

***Now listen.*** This is literally "Come now." It stands in sharp contrast to the way James has been addressing his readers. In the previous section he called them "my brothers" (3:1,11). James reverts to this more impersonal language in addressing these merchants.

***"Today or tomorrow we will go …"*** James lets us listen in on the plans of a group of businessmen. Possibly they are looking at a map together. In any case, they are planning for the future and are concerned with where they will go, how long they will stay, what they will do, and how much profit they will make. It appears to be an innocent conversation. "In trade a person has to plan ahead: Travel plans, market projections, time frames, profit forecasts are the stuff of business in all ages. Every honest merchant would plan in exactly the same way—pagan, Jew or Christian—and that is exactly the problem James has with these plans: There is absolutely nothing about their desires for the future, their use of money or their way of doing business that is any different from the rest of the world. Their worship may be exemplary, their personal morality, impeccable; but when it comes to business they think entirely on a worldly plane" (Davids, GNC).

***we will go.*** Travel by traders in the first century usually took the form of caravan or ship. There were no hard and fast time tables. Instead, one had to wait until the right transportation came along going in your direction. However, there were certain seasons when ships sailed and caravans were more likely to travel.

***carry on business.*** The word James uses here is derived from the Greek word *emporos*, from which the English word "emporium" comes. It denotes wholesale merchants who traveled from city to city, buying and selling. A different word was used to describe local peddlers who had small businesses in the bazaars. The growth of cities and the increase of trade between them during the Greco-Roman era created great opportunities for making money. In the Bible a certain distrust of traders is sometimes expressed (see Prov. 20:23; Amos 8:4–6; Rev. 18:11–20).

**4:14 *tomorrow.*** All such planning presupposes that tomorrow will unfold like any other day, when in fact, the future is anything but secure (see Prov. 27:1).

***What is your life?*** Is it not death that is the great unknown? Who can know when death will come and interrupt plans? "Their projections are made; their plans are laid. But it all hinges on a will higher than theirs, a God unconsulted in their planning. That very night disease might strike; suddenly their plans evaporate, their only trip being one on a bier to a cold grave. They are like the rich fool of Jesus' parable, who had made a large honest profit through the chance occurrences of farming. Feeling secure, he makes rational plans for a comfortable retirement. 'But God said to him, "You fool! This very night you will have to give up your life" ' (Luke 12:16–21). By thinking on the worldly plane, James' Christian business people have gained a false sense of security. They need to look death in the face and realize their lack of control over life" (Davids, GNC).

***mist.*** Hosea 13:3 says, "Therefore they will be like the morning mist, like the early dew that disappears, like chaff swirling from a threshing floor, like smoke escaping through a window."

**4:15 *"If it is the Lord's will."*** This phrase (often abbreviated D.V. after its Latin form) is not used in the Old Testament, though it was found frequently in Greek and Roman literature and is used by Paul (see Acts 18:21; 1 Cor. 4:19; 16:7). The uncertainty of the future ought not to be a terror to the Christian. Instead, it ought to force on him or her an awareness of how dependent a person is upon God, and thus move that person to a planning that involves God.

***we will live and do this or that.*** James is not ruling out planning. He says plan, but keep God in mind.

**4:16** In contrast to such prayerful planning, these Christian merchants are very proud of what they do on their own. James is not condemning international trade as such, nor the wealth it produced. (His comments on riches come in 5:1–3.) What he is concerned about is that all this is done without reference to God, in a spirit of boastful arrogance.

***boast.*** The problem with this boasting is that they are claiming to have the future under control when, in fact, it is God who holds time in his hands. These are empty claims.

***brag.*** This word originally described an itinerant quack who touted "cures" that did not work. It came to mean claiming to be able to do something that you could not do.

**4:17** Some feel that this proverb-like statement may, in fact, be a saying of Jesus that did not get recorded in the Gospel accounts. In any case, by it James points out the nature of so-called "sins of omission." In other words, it is sin when we fail to do what we ought to do. The more familiar definition is of "sins of commission" or wrongdoing (see 1 John 3:4). In other words, sinning can be both active and passive. Christians can sin by doing what they ought not to do (law-breaking); or by not doing what they know they should do (failure).

***who knows the good.*** James applies this principle to the merchants. It is not that they are cheating and stealing in the course of their business (that would be active wrongdoing). The problem is in what they fail to do. Generally James defines "the good" as acts of charity toward those in need. And certainly in the context of this letter, it would appear that these men are failing in their duty to the poor. "James, then, may be suggesting that they plan like the world because they are motivated by the world, for God has his own way to invest money: give it to the poor (Matt. 6:19–21). If they took God into account they might not be trying to increase their own standard of living; God might lead them to relieve the suffering around them, that is, to do good" (Davids, GNC).

***The uncertainty of the future ought not to be a terror to the Christian. Instead, it ought to force on him or her an awareness of how dependent a person is upon God, and thus move that person to a planning that involves God.***

# 10 Warning to the Rich—James 5:1–6

## THREE-PART AGENDA

**ICE-BREAKER**
15 Minutes

**BIBLE STUDY**
30 Minutes

**CARING TIME**
15–45 Minutes

***LEADER: To help you identify people who might form the core of a new small group (or if a new person comes to this meeting), see the listing of ice-breakers on page M7 of the center section.***

## TO BEGIN THE BIBLE STUDY TIME

(Choose 1 or 2)

1. What rich and famous person would you most like to meet?
2. What "treasure" did you collect as a kid?
3. What's the most valuable thing you have in your purse or wallet right now?

## READ SCRIPTURE & DISCUSS

(If you don't have time for all the questions in this section, conclude the Bible Study [30 min.] by answering question #7.)

1. If you inherited a million dollars, what's the first thing you would do?
2. How is success generally measured in our society? What are some of the marks of success in your community?
3. In what ways can wealth bring "misery"?
4. What are the abuses the rich committed (vv. 4–6)? How do these injustices happen today?
5. How should we manage our financial resources in such a way as to avoid the misery of wealth?

Warning to Rich Oppressors

***5** Now listen, you rich people, weep and wail because of*
*the misery that is coming upon you.* ***2*** *Your wealth has*
*rotted, and moths have eaten your clothes.* ***3*** *Your gold and*
*silver are corroded. Their corrosion will testify against you*
*and eat your flesh like fire. You have hoarded wealth in the*
*last days.* ***4*** *Look! The wages you failed to pay the workmen*
*who mowed your fields are crying out against you. The*
*cries of the harvesters have reached the ears of the Lord*
*Almighty.* ***5*** *You have lived on earth in luxury and self-indul-*
*gence. You have fattened yourselves in the day of slaugh-*
*ter.*[a] ***6*** *You have condemned and murdered innocent men,*
*who were not opposing you.*

[a]5 Or *yourselves as in a day of feasting*

6. In the past week, did you feel more devoted to God or the riches of this world?
7. If someone looked at your checkbook, what would they learn about you? In what practical ways do you feel God would have you use your financial resources?

## CARING TIME

(Choose 1 or 2 of these questions before closing in prayer. Be sure to pray for the empty chair.)

1. How are you doing at spending personal time in prayer and Bible study?
2. Who would you choose as the leader if this group “gave birth” to a new small group? Who else would you choose to be a part of the leadership core for a new group?
3. What prayer requests do you have for this week?

# Notes—James 5:1–6

**Summary.** James is still on the theme of wealth, but now he shows that riches are, indeed, a great burden when seen in eternal terms. In an unusually vivid passage, James points out the ultimate worthlessness of wealth in the face of the coming judgment. Although he is addressing the rich directly, he is also warning Christians not to covet wealth. Wealth is an illusion. It gives one a false sense of security. Not only that, it is gained at the expense of the poor, even to the extent of depriving them of their lives. And all this so that the rich can live in self-indulgent ways. In the previous passage James was concerned with the merchant class; business people who were, in this case, Christians (4:13–17). In this passage, his focus is on the landowner class who were, by and large, non-Christians.

**5:1** ***Now listen.*** James continues his impersonal mode of address. See the second note on 4:13.

***rich people.*** In the first century there was a great gulf between rich and poor. Whereas a poor laborer (as in verse 4) might have received one denarius a day as wages, a rich widow was said to have cursed the scribes because they allowed her only 400 gold denarii a day to spend on luxuries! In the face of such extravagance, the words of James take on new meaning. Peter Davids argues that the people in view here are wealthy non-Christians since James seems to reserve the word "rich" for those outside the Christian community (see 1:10 and 2:6).

***weep.*** James says that the appropriate response for these wealthy non-Christians is tears. Their luxury is only for the moment. In contrast, in 1:2 and 1:12, he urged the poor Christians to rejoice because their present suffering will pass, bringing with it great reward.

***wail.*** This is a strong word meaning "to shriek" or "howl," and is used to describe the terror that will be felt by the damned.

***the misery that is coming.*** James is referring to the future Day of Judgment, an event that will take place when the Lord returns. The noun *misery* is related (in the Greek) to the verb *grieve* used in 4:9. However, there is an important difference between the two uses. In 4:9 the grieving was self-imposed, the result of seeing one's failure, and it had a good result. Repentance opened up one to grace. But here this wretchedness results from the horror of being judged.

**5:2–3** James points to the three major forms of wealth in the first century (food, clothes, and precious metals) and describes the decay of each. Agricultural products like corn and oil will rot. Clothes will become moth-eaten. And even precious metal will corrode.

***How inappropriate it is to give your energies over to accumulating treasures when, in effect, time itself is drawing to a close. This is an example of the kind of arrogance and pride that plans boldly for the future as if a person could control what lies ahead.***

**5:2** ***clothes.*** Garments were one of the main forms of wealth in the first century. They were used as a means of payment, given as gifts, and passed on to one's children (see Gen. 45:22; Josh. 7:21; Judg. 14:12; 2 Kings 5:5; Acts 20:33).

**5:3** ***corroded.*** Pure gold and silver do not, of course, rust or corrode (though silver will tarnish). James is using hyperbole to make his point: no form of wealth will make a person immune from the final judgment.

***testify against you.*** The existence of rotten food, moth-eaten garments, and rusty coins will stand as a condemnation against the person. Instead of being stored, these goods should have been used to feed and clothe the poor.

***eat your flesh like fire.*** In a striking image, James pictures wealth as having now turned against the person and become part of the torment he or she must endure. Just as rust eats through metal, so too it will eat through the flesh of the rich (see Luke 16:19–31 and Mark 9:43).

***the last days.*** The early Christians felt that Jesus would return very shortly, to draw his people to himself and to establish his kingdom on earth. James' point is: how inappropriate it is to give your energies over to accumulating treasures when, in effect, time itself is drawing to a close. This is an example of the kind of arrogance and pride that plans boldly for the future as if a person could control what lies ahead (see 4:14–16). "The rich gather and invest as if they or their descendants will live forever, yet the last days, the beginning of the end, are already here. James sees as tragic figures well-dressed men and women pondering investments over excellent meals; they act as if they were winners, but in reality have lost the only game that matters" (Davids, GNC).

**5:4–6** James now gets very specific as he details how it is that these folks were able to accumulate such wealth. In particular he points to the injustices leveled against those who worked on the farms.

**5:4 *Look!*** James will not let them turn away from this stinging condemnation. They must see things as they are. They must face the reality of their own injustice.

**5:4 *wages you failed to pay.*** If a laborer was not given his wages at the end of the day, his family would go hungry the next day. The Old Testament insists that it is wrong to withhold wages. A worker was to be paid immediately. "Despite a host of Old Testament laws (Lev. 19:13; Deut. 24:14–15), ways were found to withhold payments (e.g., Jer. 22:13; Mal. 3:5). One might withhold them until the end of the harvest season to keep the worker coming back, grasp at a technicality to show that the contract was not fulfilled, or just be too tired to pay that night. If the poor worker complained, the landlord could blacklist him; if he went to court the rich had the better lawyers. James pictures the money in the pockets of the rich, money that should have been paid to the laborers, crying out for justice" (Davids, GNC).

***the workmen.*** In Palestine, day laborers were used to plant and harvest the crops. They were cheaper than slaves, since if a slave converted to Judaism, he or she had to be freed in the sabbatical year.

***"James sees as tragic figures well-dressed men and women pondering investments over excellent meals; they act as if they were winners, but in reality have lost the only game that matters."***

***fields.*** The Greek word means "estates." These were the large tracts of land owned by the very wealthy.

***crying out.*** This is a word used to describe the wild, incoherent cry of an animal.

***the Lord Almighty.*** This means literally "The Lord of Sabbaoth" or "Lord of Hosts," i.e., the commander of the heavenly armies. This is an unusual title, found at only one other place in the New Testament (and there it is a quote—Rom. 9:29). James has probably drawn the title from Isaiah 5:7,9,16,24—a chapter whose concerns parallel his own in this passage.

**5:5 *luxury.*** In contrast to the hunger of the laborers is the soft and easy living of the landowners (see Amos 6:1–7).

***self-indulgence.*** "To live in lewdness and lasciviousness and wanton riotousness" (Barclay). Not just luxury but vice is in view here.

***day of slaughter.*** Cattle were pampered and fattened for one purpose only: to be slaughtered. On the day when this took place a great feast was held.

**5:6** There is yet another accusation against the rich: they use their wealth and power to oppress the poor, even to the point of death.

# 11 Patience in Suffering—James 5:7–12

## THREE-PART AGENDA

**ICE-BREAKER**
15 Minutes

**BIBLE STUDY**
30 Minutes

**CARING TIME**
15–45 Minutes

***LEADER: Has your group discussed its plans on what to study after this course is finished? What about the mission project described on page M6 in the center section?***

## TO BEGIN THE BIBLE STUDY TIME

(Choose 1 or 2)

1. In which "waiting" situation are you usually the most impatient: At a stoplight? In a slow-moving line? In anticipation of vacation?
2. As a kid, what is a project you worked on that required a great deal of perseverance?
3. If you were a farmer, what crop would you like to raise?

## READ SCRIPTURE & DISCUSS

(If you don't have time for all the questions in this section, conclude the Bible Study [30 min.] by answering question #7.)

1. What event are you patiently (or impatiently) waiting for? What grade would you give yourself on the virtue of patience?
2. What does James call Christians to wait for patiently?
3. What are you looking forward to the most about "the Lord's coming" (v. 8)?

Patience in Suffering

***7Be patient, then, brothers, until the Lord's coming. See how the farmer waits for the land to yield its valuable crop and how patient he is for the autumn and spring rains. 8You too, be patient and stand firm, because the Lord's coming is near. 9Don't grumble against each other, brothers, or you will be judged. The Judge is standing at the door!***

***10Brothers, as an example of patience in the face of suffering, take the prophets who spoke in the name of the Lord. 11As you know, we consider blessed those who have persevered. You have heard of Job's perseverance and have seen what the Lord finally brought about. The Lord is full of compassion and mercy.***

***12Above all, my brothers, do not swear—not by heaven or by earth or by anything else. Let your "Yes" be yes, and your "No," no, or you will be condemned.***

4. How are Christians to behave during this waiting time before the Lord's return?
5. How are you at keeping your word—letting your " 'Yes' be yes, and your 'No,' no" (v. 12)?
6. Have you been feeling more of God's judgment or mercy in the past week? How does this passage encourage you?
7. Where in your life do you need God's help to patiently persevere?

## CARING TIME

(Answer all the questions that follow, then take prayer requests and close in prayer.)

1. Next week will be your last session in this study. How would you like to celebrate: A dinner? A party? Other?
2. What is the next step for this group: Start a new group? Continue with another study?
3. What would you like to share with the group for prayer this week?

(If the group plans to continue, see the back inside cover of this book for what's available from Serendipity.)

# Notes—James 5:7–12

**Summary.** James' argument is finished. He has said what he wants to say about testing (and temptation), about wisdom (and speech), and about riches (and generosity). Now all that remains is for him to conclude his book by summarizing his points. However, he does not do this in a neat, systematic way. Rather, he simply alludes to each theme in the midst of offering final encouragement to the church in Jerusalem.

**5:7–11** It has been very difficult for the church in Jerusalem. The times are hard. There is famine. There is poverty. Being Christians, they have received little of the general relief donated by wealthy Jewish aristocrats living outside Palestine. Then there is the persecution which has pushed them down even further. So they are weary. When will the trials end? When will Christ return? Their hard situation has worn them down so that they are slipping from Christ's way into the ways of the world. "Hold on," James says, "stand firm, be like Job. Jesus will return." Part of this "holding on" involves not taking oaths. They are to be people of their word, not like the people of the world who used (abused) words to get their own way.

**5:7–8** James begins this concluding section by summarizing his ideas about testing.

**5:7** ***patient.*** This word (and its derivatives) are the most frequently used words in the passage. The basic idea is that of *patient waiting.* It is related to the endurance that James commended in 1:3 ("perseverance"), though patience connotes a more passive holding on than the active endurance of chapter 1. This word carries with it the idea of "self-restraint in the face of injustice" like that which he catalogued in 5:4–6 (failure to be paid, being used to bring opulence to a few while personally being forced to live in poverty, abuse in the courts, murder). The opposite response to such patience would be retaliation or vengeance (see Rom. 2:4 and 1 Peter 3:20).

***brothers.*** James has shifted back into this personal form of address (as in 4:11 and elsewhere), away from his impersonal tone in 4:13 and 5:1. The whole atmosphere of the passage has changed from that of warning and command (in 4:13–5:6) to encouragement and gentle instruction.

***until.*** Such patient waiting on the part of the poor is possible because they know that an event is coming that will radically change their situation, namely the Lord's return.

***the Lord's coming.*** There are three words in the New Testament used to describe the second coming of Jesus. The first is *epiphaneia* (English: "epiphany"). It describes the appearance of a god or the ascent to the throne of an emperor (see 2 Tim. 4:1). The second word is *apokalupsis* (English: apocalypse) and means "unveiling" or "revelation" (see 1 Peter 1:7,13). The third word which is used here is *parousia.* It describes the invasion of a country or the arrival of a king (Barclay). Taken together, these three words give the sense of what will occur when Christ returns. Jesus first came to this planet in secret as a little baby in Bethlehem. When he comes a second time it will be in great and obvious power as the rightful King. In great glory he will ascend his throne and claim his people.

***See how the farmer waits.*** In due course, the rains will come. In the meantime, the farmer can do nothing to hasten or delay their arrival. He must simply wait for the gift of rain.

***for the land to yield.*** Likewise, he must wait for the land to give forth a crop. Once he has sowed his seed (apart from pulling out weeds and keeping birds and animals away), there is nothing the farmer can do. Growth, too, is a gift.

***valuable.*** This was literally his most precious possession. Without a crop he would have nothing to sell or barter. Even worse, he and his family would starve.

***rains.*** The fall rain comes in late October or early November and was necessary to prepare the hard ground for sowing and to enable the seed to germinate. The spring rains in April and May were vital for the grain to ripen and mature.

**5:8** ***stand firm.*** While waiting, the temptation will be to slip into inappropriate survival modes—specifically in this case, that of adopting the methods of the world (e.g., revenge). The longer they wait, the stronger the temptation to doubt the Second Coming, and even to doubt the Christian faith itself. They must resist these temptations.

> *God does not enjoy seeing people suffer.*

***near.*** The common feeling in the New Testament days was that the Lord's return was imminent—any day now (see Rom. 13:11–12).

**5:9** James now touches on the theme of speech.

***grumble.*** This word is literally "groan." While groaning in the face of suffering is appropriate (see Mark 7:34 and Rom. 8:23), groaning at one another is not! While they wait, they are not to bicker and find fault. Such grumbling can easily develop in a tough situation in which people cannot vent their frustrations at those causing the problem, so the frustration is directed at those who are around them.

***you will be judged.*** Grumbling against others is a form of judgment so this reference may be to the teaching of Jesus: "Do not judge, or you too will be judged. For in the same way you judge others, you will be judged, and with the measure you use, it will be measured to you" (Matt. 7:1–2). This is likely since James frequently refers to the Sermon on the Mount. Or, James may have in mind the Day of Judgment which will occur at the Second Coming.

**5:10–11** From the theme of speech, James moves back to the theme of trials and tests.

**5:10 *take the prophets.*** James does not have to mention by name all the men and women who spoke truth in God's name and suffered for it. In this oral culture, versed in Scripture, all he has to do is to make a reference and the people will think of the stories by themselves.

**5:11 *persevered.*** At this point, James shifts from the more passive word "patience" to the idea of active endurance of suffering, a concept which describes Job's experience.

***finally brought about.*** But in the end, God blessed Job with far more than he had at the beginning of his trials (Job 42:10–17). The implications of this are clear: if they will hold on ("stand firm"), their reward too will be great.

***The Lord is full of compassion and mercy.*** An allusion to Psalm 103:8 or 111:4. God does not enjoy seeing people suffer. He will intervene in the fullness of time.

**5:12** James shifts back to the tongue. This is the first of a series of commandments by which he will end his letter, each of which have to do with how to live while waiting for Jesus to return.

***swear.*** The issue is not that of using foul language but of taking an oath to guarantee a promise. The extraordinary amount of oathtaking in those days

> *Christians have no need for oaths. They are expected to speak only what is true.*

was an indication of how widespread lying and cheating was. (Honest people need no oaths.) In Jewish society, an oath containing the name of God was binding, since God was then seen as a partner in the transaction. But when God's name was not mentioned the oath was not binding. "The result of this was that men became experts in evasive swearing; and it became a matter of skill and sharp practice to find an oath which was not binding" (Barclay).

***"Yes" be yes.*** Christians have no need for oaths. They are expected to speak only what is true. Once again, James is alluding to a saying of Jesus, who taught the same thing when it came to oaths (see Matt. 5:33–37).

# 12 Prayer of Faith—James 5:13–20

## THREE-PART AGENDA

**ICE-BREAKER**
15 Minutes

**BIBLE STUDY**
30 Minutes

**CARING TIME**
15–45 Minutes

***LEADER: Check page M7 of the center section for a good ice-breaker for this last session.***

## TO BEGIN THE BIBLE STUDY TIME

(Choose 1 or 2)

1. What is your family's home remedy for a cold?
2. Do you feel more like praying or singing today and why?
3. When you get into a situation where you're "in over your head," who do you call for help?

## READ SCRIPTURE & DISCUSS

(If you don't have time for all the questions in this section, conclude the Bible Study [30 min.] by answering question #7.)

1. How has this group, or someone in the group, been a blessing to you over the course of this study?
2. Who is someone you admire as a person of prayer? Who is someone you pray for regularly?
3. According to this passage, what should you do when you are: In trouble? Happy? Sick? How apt are you to do any of these?
4. How is confession and prayer a part of the healing process? What is the connection between the physical and spiritual areas of our lives?

The Prayer of Faith

***13**Is any one of you in trouble? He should pray. Is anyone
happy? Let him sing songs of praise. **14**Is any one of you
sick? He should call the elders of the church to pray over
him and anoint him with oil in the name of the Lord. **15**And
the prayer offered in faith will make the sick person well;
the Lord will raise him up. If he has sinned, he will be forgiven. **16**Therefore confess your sins to each other and pray
for each other so that you may be healed. The prayer of a
righteous man is powerful and effective.*

***17**Elijah was a man just like us. He prayed earnestly that it
would not rain, and it did not rain on the land for three and
a half years. **18**Again he prayed, and the heavens gave rain,
and the earth produced its crops.*

***19**My brothers, if one of you should wander from the truth
and someone should bring him back, **20**remember this:
Whoever turns a sinner from the error of his way will save
him from death and cover over a multitude of sins.*

5. What's the closest you've come to wandering from the faith? Who or what helped bring you back?
6. In this study of the book of James, what has been the key thing you have learned?
7. On a scale of 1 (baby steps) to 10 (giant leaps), how has your relationship with God progressed over the last three months?

## CARING TIME

(Answer all the questions that follow, then take prayer requests and close in prayer.)

1. What will you remember most about this group?
2. What has the group decided to do next? What is the next step for you personally?
3. How would you like the group to continue to pray for you?

# Notes—James 5:13–20

**Summary.** In literary epistles such as this one (according to Peter Davids), it is customary to end with three items: an oath, a health wish, and the purpose for writing. James has each of these. In 5:12, oaths are mentioned (though not in the traditional way). James does not offer an oath to guarantee the truth of this letter. He rejects all oaths! In verses 13–18 there is a health wish, as James instructs them in how to obtain health through prayer. And then finally, he sums up the purpose of his letter in verses 19–20. His aim has been to warn sinners of their erroneous ways.

**5:13–18** The theme of this section is prayer. Prayer is the form of speech that James commends most highly in his letter. However, James also identifies two other forms of speech which ought to characterize Christians: singing (v. 13) and confession of sins (v. 16). Such proper speech contrasts with the two forms of improper speech identified in the previous session: grumbling (5:8) and oath-taking (5:12). In this way, James summarizes his teaching on speech while at the same time extending it to new areas.

***James is quite clear about the source of the healing. It is not the oil, it is not the laying on of hands by the elders, nor is it even prayer in some sort of magical sense. It is God who heals.***

**5:13 *trouble.*** James does not define the nature of the trouble. However, in the course of his letter he has pointed out a variety of troubles facing the church: favoritism (2:1–4), exploitation and litigation (2:5–7; 5:1–6), lack of the physical necessities of life (2:15), slander and cursing (3:9–12; 4:11–12), and community disharmony (3:13–4:3). He has also just alluded to the persecution of the prophets (5:10–11) and to the physical, mental and spiritual suffering of Job (5:11). These are troubles aplenty!

***pray.*** The first response to all these troubles ought to be prayer (see Psalm 30; 50:15; 91:15).

***happy.*** James knows that life is not one unrelenting misery. There are times of joy and these too call for a verbal response, in this case, singing.

***sing.*** The Christian church has long been noted for its singing. In his letter to the Roman Emperor Trajan describing the Christian sect, Pliny the governor of Bithynia wrote "that they were in the habit of meeting on a certain, fixed day before it was light, when they sang in alternate verses a hymn to Christ as God" (see also 1 Cor. 14:15,26; Eph. 5:19; Col. 3:16).

**5:14–15** There is a long tradition of faith healing in the Christian church. Jesus and the apostles healed the sick. In the second century, Irenaeus wrote of healings by means of laying on of hands. In the third century, Tertulian wrote that the Roman Emperor Alexander Severus was healed by anointing.

**5:14 *sick.*** It is one thing to be persecuted, to be hungry, or to fight with other church members. These problems stem from the evil that is in the world. But illness is another matter. It is not something anybody else does to you. Especially in the first century, illness made one feel so vulnerable. What could you do? Where could you go for help? James has an answer to this question.

***call the elders.*** Illness was to be dealt with in the context of the Christian community. The elders—the council that ran the church—were to be called to minister to the ill person. They had two things to do: to pray over the person and to anoint them with oil.

***anoint him with oil.*** When a Jew was ill, he or she first went to a rabbi to be anointed with oil. Oil was used not only for ritual purposes but for cleaning wounds, for paralysis, and for toothaches. In this case, the olive oil is not being used as a medicine but as a part of the healing prayer (see Mark 6:13 and Luke 10:34).

**5:15 *prayer offered in faith.*** James has discussed this kind of prayer already (see 1:5–8 and 4:1–3). His point is that "without the life of commitment to God that the prayer expresses, it will be ineffectual. The faith lies in the elders, not in the sick person (about whose faith nothing is said). The elders' faith is critical: If something 'goes wrong' it is they, not the sick person, who bear the onus" (Davids, GNC).

***the Lord will raise him up.*** James is quite clear about the source of the healing. It is not the oil, it is not the laying on of hands by the elders, nor is it even prayer in some sort of magical sense. It is God who heals.

***sinned.*** Traditional Judaism maintained that there was a connection between sin and illness: "No sick person is cured of his disease until all his sins are forgiven him" (Babylonian Talmud). In this sense, healing would be a confirmation that God had also forgiven the sins that were confessed (see Mark 2:1–12). Though James does not teach an inevitable connection between sin and illness, he suggests that at times this may be the case, much as modern medicine has recognized that illness is often a product of wrong living (psychosomatic illness).

**5:16 *Therefore.*** James will summarize his teaching concerning healing and prayer. Public confession and believing prayer are key to what he says.

***confess your sins.*** Confessing your sins to one another removes barriers between people and promotes honesty in the Christian community.

***to each other.*** This is not an action to be taken only when one is ill (and then only with the elders). Public confession of sins is for everyone.

***powerful and effective.*** It is not that prayer is an independent force (like magic incantations). Prayer is directed to *God*, who is all-powerful and who works in this world.

**5:17 *Elijah.*** Though in the story told in 1 Kings 17 and 18, no direct mention is made of Elijah praying, the rabbis taught that the words in 1 Kings 17:1, "whom I serve" (which is translated literally "standing before God") and the words in 1 Kings 18:42, "bent down to the ground," refer to prayer.

***man just like us.*** Elijah was not a plastic saint more comfortable in another world than this one. He knew depression, despair and doubt just as did the Christians in the Jerusalem church (see 1 Kings 19). And yet, God answered his prayer in a mighty way. Perhaps James realizes at this point that he could be misinterpreted in what he had said about prayer and be understood to mean that only a special few could pray and expect God to answer. (In verse 15 he mentioned "prayer offered in faith," and he has already said a lot about what real faith is. And in verse 16 it is the prayer of a "righteous man" that avails.) Here he makes it clear that all Christians can pray like this, not just prophets or saints.

> ***Christian truth captivates not only the mind, but one's whole life, including how one lives.***

**5:18 *the earth produced its crops.*** In 5:7, rain necessary to grow crops is mentioned as one of those things a farmer cannot control. He must just wait patiently for it to rain. But now James points out that this is not the whole story. God controls the rain and Christians can pray to him to bring rain. By implication, while patiently enduring their troubles, Christians can pray in confidence to God about them.

**5:19–20** James concludes his letter by summarizing its purpose.

**5:19 *wander.*** Christian truth captivates not only the mind, but one's whole life, including how one lives. This is the point of James' letter. Hence James can speak about wandering from Christian truth, presumably into other styles of living. It is not primarily doctrinal deviation that has concerned James. It is how one lives.

## Notes (cont.)

***truth.*** "Christian truth is something which must be done. Christian truth is not only an intellectual exercise; it is not only something which is the object of the search of the mind; it is not an academic affair; it is not a matter of knowledge and of opinion, or argument and of debate. Christian truth is always moral truth; it is always truth which issues in action; it is not only a process of the mind, it is also a thing to be done. Christian truth is not something to which a man must submit only his mind; it is something to which he has to submit his whole life. It is not only something by which he thinks, it is also, and even more, something by which he lives. Christian truth is not the affair only of the study circle and the discussion group: Christian truth is the affair of life" (Barclay).

**5:20 *turns.*** This word can be translated "converts" when it is applied to unbelievers. "James holds out an assurance of blessing both to the converted and to the converter; the act of conversion is of mutual benefit: the man who is turned from error is thereby delivered from death, and the man who reclaims him experiences himself forgiveness of his sins. It is, of course, assumed that the man who takes it upon himself to reclaim his fellow from error will be conscious of errors of his own for which he too stands in need of forgiveness" (Laws).

# Acknowledgments

In writing these notes, use has been made of the standard exegetical tools—Bible dictionaries, lexicons, word studies, background studies and a variety of commentaries. In this regard, particular note must be made of two books by Peter H. Davids. These were published after the first draft of the manuscript had been completed. In the revision process they proved to be invaluable, clearing up a host of questions, giving a feel for the overall structure of the book, and in general serving as models of good scholarship linked to passionate concern for the truth of what is in the book of James. One of Dr. Davids' books is written for a general audience and it would be an excellent resource to use along with this material. It is entitled simply *James* and is part of the *Good News Commentary* series published in 1983 by Harper and Row (abbreviated in the study notes as GNC). The second volume is a more technical study and requires some familiarity with Greek. It will be of special value to the pastor who is teaching this course. Its title is *Commentary on James* and it is part of the *New International Greek Testament Commentary* series, published in 1982 by the William B. Eerdmans Publishing Company (abbreviated in the study notes as NIGTC).

Two other commentaries were of special value: *The Epistle of James* by Sophie Laws (*Harper's New Testament Commentaries*), New York: Harper and Row, 1980; and *The Letters of James and Peter* by William Barclay (*The Daily Study Bible*), Philadelphia: The Westminster Press, 1960. Both the Laws and Barclay volumes contained a wealth of historical detail and background data.

Reference was also made to *The Epistle of James* by James Adamson (*The New International Commentary on the New Testament*), Grand Rapids: William B. Eerdmans Publishing Co., 1976; *James* by Marilyn Kunz and Catherine Schell (Neighborhood Bible Studies), Wheaton: Tyndale House Publishers; *The Tests of Faith* by J.A. Motyer, London: InterVarsity Press, 1970; *The Epistles of James, Peter, and Jude* by Bo Reicke (*The Anchor Bible*), Garden City, NY: Doubleday & Co., 1964; *A Critical and Exegetical Commentary on the Epistle of St. James* by James Hardy Ropes (*The International Critical Commentary*), Edinburgh: T. & T. Clark, 1978; *The General Epistle of James* by R.V.G. Tasker (*Tyndale New Testament Commentaries*), London: The Tyndale Press, 1956; and *The Letters of John and James* by R. R. Williams (*The Cambridge Bible Commentary*), Cambridge at the University Press, 1965.

# Caring Time Notes